HOLMAN
BOOK OF
BIBLICAL CHARTS,
MAPS, AND
RECONSTRUCTIONS

HOLMAN
BOOK OF BIBLICAL CHARTS, MAPS, AND RECONSTRUCTIONS

GENERAL EDITOR
MARSHA A. ELLIS SMITH

MANAGING EDITOR
JUNE SWANN

CONTRIBUTING EDITORS
TRENT C. BUTLER
CHRISTOPHER L. CHURCH
DAVID S. DOCKERY

BROADMAN & HOLMAN PUBLISHERS

Nashville, Tennessee

ISBN: 1-55819-359-6

Bible passages are from the Holy Bible,
New International Version,
copyright © 1973, 1978, 1984
by International Bible Society.
Used by permission.

Printed in the United States of America
by Arcata Graphics Company
of Kingsport, Tennessee.

4 5 6 7 02 01 00 99
Q

EDITORIAL FOREWORD

The word of God is the very foundation of our lives. And to know His word we must read and study it. With this in mind, we have developed the *Holman Book of Biblical Charts, Maps, and Reconstructions* with a two-fold purpose:

(1) To provide a tool for use in personal Bible study; and

(2) To provide a teaching aid for small group Bible study.

Many Bible study tools—dictionaries, handbooks, encyclopedias, and study Bibles—contain various charts, maps, and artists' reconstructions. The problem we wanted to solve is how to keep a book open to a helpful visual and yet continue following the text of the volume as you study. Our answer is the book you now hold in your hands. You can prop this volume open on your desk while you are at home studying or you can display it opened to a particular page on a table, chair, or even on the floor when you are leading a small group Bible study. If the visual is in a vertical page design, find the desired pages and set the book open at an angle. The hard cover material and wire binding will enable it to stand alone. If the visual you want to use is in a horizontal page design, turn the covers all the way back and set it on the table as you would a flip chart. The cover and binding will support this usage as well. A few of the horizontal charts are two pages in length and will need some assistance to be shown. We think this format provides a needed medium for use with those groups not quite large enough to need a wall chart but too large to look over your shoulder at the pages of a book.

The layout includes three major divisions—one for each type of visual. Within each division the pages are grouped under "general" (or "contemporary" in the maps division), "Old Testament," and "New Testament." Within each of these sections the titles are grouped in a loose alphabetical arrangement. Color bars (the "quicktab" system introduced in the *Holman Bible Dictionary*) in the margins of the pages provide easy access to each of the three divisions.

The Cross References located on pages 167-169 is a normal alphabetical index to all titles and page numbers in this volume. However, it also provides information on where to look in the *Holman Bible Dictionary, Holman Bible Handbook*, and *Disciple's Study Bible* to find related articles and background information for each of these titles. We want you to be able to interrelate all of your Holman Bible reference tools.

We pray that the *Holman Book of Biblical Charts, Maps, and Reconstructions* will provide a useful source of background information to assist you in your study and sharing of God's message through His written Word.

Marsha A. Ellis Smith

PRODUCTION STAFF

GENERAL EDITOR
MARSHA A. ELLIS SMITH

MANAGING EDITOR
JUNE SWANN

CONTRIBUTING EDITORS
TRENT C. BUTLER
CHRISTOPHER L. CHURCH • DAVID S. DOCKERY

PRODUCTION TEAM
DANIEL HALPIN • RENA HARRIS
TRINA HOLLISTER • BOB MORRISON
WENDELL OVERSTREET • WENDY SCOTT
WILLIAM R. SMITH • DEAN SUTHERLAND

ARTISTS
ERNIE COUCH/CONSULTX
JOAN ALFORD • ED MAKSIMOWITZ
TOM SEALE • DAVID SHEPHERD
STEPHEN SMITH

ART CONTRIBUTORS
Holman Bible Publishers, Nashville, TN. All charts and maps excluding those listed below.

Broadman & Holman Publishers, Nashville, TN. pp. 48-49; 107.

The Foreign Mission Board of the Southern Baptist Convention, Richmond, VA.
Chart, p. 28; and chart/map (Nancy C. Wogsland, artist), pp. 108-109.

Bill Latta, Nashville, TN. All reconstructions.

TABLE OF CONTENTS

Editorial Foreword.. 5

Production Staff 6

Charts... 9

General Charts 11
    52-Week Bible Reading Plan 13
    Ancient Versions of the Biblical Text... 14
    Ancient Number Systems.. 15
    The Apocrypha 16
    Archaeological Periods of Palestine... 17
    The Bible in English 18
    The Books of the Bible 20
    Comparison of Lists of the Old Testament Books 21
    Denominational Perspectives on Major Doctrines 22
    The Hebrew Canon of the Old Testament 24
    Names of God... 25
    New Testament Apocrypha 26
    Prayers of the Bible... 27
    Religions of the World 28
    Stages in the Development of the New Testament Canon 29
    Table of Weights and Measures... 30
    Time Line... 32

Old Testament Charts 41
    Abraham, The Family of.. 43
    Assyrian Rulers.. 44
    Babylonian Rulers/Persian Rulers... 45
    The Characteristics of God Presented in the Psalms.. 46
    Cities of Joshua's Conquest 48
    Covenants and Law Codes 50
    David, The Family of.. 51
    Human Characteristics Presented in the Psalms.. 52
    The Jewish Calendar... 54
    Jewish Feasts and Festivals... 56
    Judges of the Old Testament/Life of Abraham 57
    Messianic Prophecies of the Old Testament... 58
    Musical Instruments of the Old Testament 60
    Priests in the Old Testament.. 61
    The Prophets in History 62
    Queens of the Old Testament/The Return from Exile 63
    Rulers of Old Testament Pagan Nations 64
    Rulers of Israel and Judah 65
    Sacrificial System/The Ten Plagues of Egypt 66
    The Ten Commandments.. 67

New Testament Charts.. 69
    Controversy Stories in Mark 71
    Disciples of Jesus... 72
    Discourses of Jesus 73
    Doctrinal Emphases in the Letters of Paul... 74
    Harmony of the Gospels... 76
    Early Caesars of Rome.. 84
    The Hasmonean Dynasty/The Herodian Rulers 85
    "I AM" Sayings in the Gospel of John/Jesus' Ministry
            as Fulfillment of Scripture in Matthew 86
    Jesus in Scripture, Titles for 87
    Major Jewish Sects in the New Testament.. 88
    Millennial Perspectives on Revelation 92
    Miracles of Jesus... 95

Parables of Jesus 96
Paul's List of Spiritual Gifts 98
Paul's Mission Travels and Letters/The Seven Signs
    in John 99
Ten Major Sermons in Acts 100
Themes in Luke 101

Maps 103

Contemporary Maps 105
Bible Lands Today 107
World A: The Unreached World 108

Old Testament Maps 111
The Assyrian Empire 113
The Conquest 114
David's Flight from Saul/Jerusalem After the Exile 115
Divided Monarchies 116
The Empire of Alexander the Great 117
The Exodus Route 118
Kingdom of David and Solomon 119
The Kingdom of Saul 120
The Medo-Babylonian Empire 121
The Persian Empire 122
The Route of Abraham 123
The Twelve Tribes 124

New Testament Maps 125
Palestine in New Testament Times 127
Paul's First Missionary Journey 128
Paul's Second Missionary Journey 129
Paul's Third Missionary Journey 130
Paul's Journey to Rome 131
The Roman Empire 132
The Seven Churches of Asia 133

Reconstructions 135

Old Testament Reconstructions 137
Ark of the Covenant 139
Eighth-century B.C. Hebrew Home 140
Jerusalem During the Time of David 141
Solomon's Temple 142
Solomon's Temple—Cut-Away View 143
Tabernacle of the Israelites 144
Ziggurat 145

New Testament Reconstructions 147
Athens of the First Century 148
Caesarea Maritima 149
First-Century Hebrew Home 150
First-Century Synagogue 151
First-Century Wine Press 152
Herod's Temple 153
Herod's Temple—Floor Plan 154
Herod's Winter Palace at Jericho 156
Jericho, New Testament 157
Jerusalem in the Time of Jesus 158
Pool of Bethesda 160
Roman Archer's Machine/Roman Battering Ram 161
Roman Siege Tower 162
Temple of Artemis 163

Cross References and Map Index 165

Cross References 167

Map Index 170

CHARTS

GENERAL CHARTS

52-WEEK BIBLE READING PLAN

Guides the reader through the Old Testament once and
the New Testament twice in one year.

1 — Genesis 1–26
2 — Genesis 27–50
3 — Matthew
4 — Mark
5 — Exodus 1–21
6 — Exodus 22–40
7 — Luke
8 — John
9 — Leviticus
10 — Acts
11 — Numbers 1–18
12 — Numbers 19–36
13 — Romans; Galatians
14 — 1, 2 Corinthians
15 — Deuteronomy 1–17
16 — Deuteronomy 18–34
17 — Ephesians; Philippians;
Colossians;
1, 2 Thessalonians;
1, 2 Timothy; Titus;
Philemon
18 — Hebrews; James;
1, 2 Peter
19 — Joshua
20 — 1, 2, 3 John; Jude;
Revelation
21 — Judges; Ruth
22 — Job 1–31
23 — Job 32–42; Ecclesiastes;
Song of Solomon
24 — 1 Samuel
25 — 2 Samuel
26 — Psalms 1–50
27 — 1 Kings

28 — 2 Kings
29 — Psalms 51–100
30 — 1 Chronicles
31 — 2 Chronicles
32 — Psalms 101–150
33 — Ezra; Nehemiah; Esther
34 — Proverbs
35 — Matthew
36 — Isaiah 1–35
37 — Isaiah 36–66
38 — Mark
39 — Luke
40 — Jeremiah 1–29
41 — Jeremiah 30–52;
Lamentations
42 — John
43 — Acts
44 — Ezekiel 1–24
45 — Ezekiel 25–48
46 — Romans; Galatians
47 — 1, 2 Corinthians
48 — Daniel; Hosea; Joel; Amos
49 — Ephesians; Philippians;
Colossians;
1, 2 Thessalonians;
1, 2 Timothy; Titus;
Philemon
50 — Obadiah; Jonah; Micah;
Nahum; Habakkuk;
Zephaniah; Haggai;
Zechariah; Malachi
51 — Hebrews; James;
1, 2 Peter
52 — 1, 2, 3 John; Jude; Revelation

ANCIENT VERSIONS OF BIBLICAL TEXT

300 B.C.

GREEK (The Septuagint—Old Testament in Greek)

200 B.C.

100 B.C.

ARAMAIC (The Targums—paraphrases of the Old Testament, originally oral and later in written form)

0

A.D. 100

-14-

GREEK (Various translations by Aquila, Theodotion, Symmachus, Origen, Lucian, and Hesychius)

A.D. 200

■ **Tatian's Diatessaron** (a harmony of the four Gospels in Greek and Syriac)

SYRIAC (Old Syriac, Peshitta, and others)

LATIN (Old Latin translations and Jerome's Vulgate)

A.D. 300

COPTIC (Sahidic, Boharic, and others)

A.D. 400

■ **GOTHIC** (by Bishop Ulfilas)

ARMENIAN

■ **GEORGIAN**

A.D. 500

ETHIOPIC

A.D. 600

A.D. 700

ANCIENT NUMBER SYSTEMS

AMERICAN	SUMERIAN	EARLY EGYPTIAN (HIEROGLYPHIC)	LATER EGYPTIAN (HIERATIC)	CANAANITE (and PHOENICIAN)	POST-EXILIC HEBREW	EARLY GREEK	LATER GREEK (IONIC)	ANCIENT ROMAN (LATIN)
1	˅ (or ˅)	I	I	I	א	I	A	I
2	˅˅ (or ˅˅)	II	⊰	II	⊐	II	B	II
3	˅˅˅ (or ˅˅˅)	III	⫶⫶	III	⅂	III	Γ	III
4	˅˅˅˅ (or ˅˅˅˅)	IIII	⫶⫶⫶	IIII	⅃⅃	IIII	Δ	III (or IV)
5	˅˅˅ (or ˅˅˅)	IIIII	˒˅	II III	Γ	⌐	E	V
6	˅˅˅ (or ˅˅˅)	III III	˒˒˅	III III	⊤	⌐I	F	VI
7	˅˅˅˅ (or ˅˅˅˅)	IIII III	⊐	I IIII	⊓	⌐II	Z	VII
8	˅˅˅˅ (or ˅˅˅˅)	IIII IIII	⊐	II IIII	⍟	⌐III	H	VIII
9	˅˅˅˅˅ (or ˅˅˅˅˅)	IIII IIIII	⫶⫶⫶	III IIIII	⊙	⌐IIII	Θ	VIIII (or IX)
10	⟨ (or ◣)	∩	∧	⌐	˙	Δ	I	X
20	⟨⟨ (or ◣◣)	∩∩	˄	ϵ	⊓	ΔΔ	K	XX
50			⌐		⅂		N	L
100		℮	⌐		φ	H	P	C
200		℮℮			⅃	HH	Σ	CC
1,000		𓆼	℔			X	⁄A	M

-15-

THE APOCRYPHA

TITLES (listed alphabetically)	APPROX-IMATE DATES	LITERARY TYPES	THEMES	IN SEPTUAGINT?	IN ROMAN CATHOLIC CANON?
Baruch	150-60 B.C.	Wisdom & narrative (composite)	Praise of wisdom, law, promise of hope, opposition to idolatry	Yes	Yes
Bel and the Dragon	100 B.C.	Detective narrative at end of Daniel	Opposition to idolatry	Yes	Yes
Ecclesiasticus (Wisdom of Jesus Sirach)	180 B.C. in Hebrew; 132 B.C. Greek Translation	Wisdom, patriotism; temple worship; retribution; free will	Obedience to law, praise of patriarchs, value of wisdom	Yes	Yes
I Esdras	150	History (621–458 B.C.)	Proper worship; power of truth	Yes	No
2 Esdras	A.D. 100	Apocalypse with Christian preface and epilog	Pre-existent, dying Messiah: punishment for sin; salvation in future; inspiration; divine justice; evil	No	No
Additions to Esther (103 verses)	114 B.C.	Religious amplification	Prayer; worship; revelation; God's activity; providence	Yes	Yes
Letter of Jeremiah	317 B.C.	Homily added to Baruch based on Jer 29	Condemn idolatry	Yes	Yes
Judith	200-100 B.C.	Historical novel	Obedience to law; prayer; fasting; true worship patriotism	Yes	Yes
1 Maccabees	90 B.C.	History (180–134 B.C.)	God works in normal human events; legitimate Hasmonean kings	Yes	Yes
2 Maccabees	90 B.C.	History (180–161 B.C.)	Resurrection; creation from nothing; miracles; punishment for sin; martyrdom; temple; angels	Yes	Yes
3 Maccabees	75 B.C.	Festival legend	Deliverance of faithful; angels	Some mss.	No
4 Maccabees	10 B.C.; A.D. 20-54	Philosophical treatise based on 2 Macc 6–7	Power of reason over emotions; faithfulness to law; martyrdom; immortality	Some mss.	No
Prayer of Azariah and Song of Three Young Men	100 B.C.	Liturgy; hymn & additions to Dan 3:23	Praise; God's response to prayer	Yes	Yes
Prayer of Manasseh	200-1 B.C.	Prayer of penitence based on 2 Kgs 21:10-17 2 Chr 33:11-19	Prayer of repentance	Yes	No
Psalm 151	?	Victory hymn	Praise to God who uses young & inexperienced	Yes	No
Susanna	100 B.C.	Detective story at end of Daniel	Daniel's wisdom; God's vindication of faithfulness	Yes	Yes
Tobit	200-100 B.C.	Folktale	Temple attendance; tithing; charity; prayer; obedience to Jewish law; guardian angel; divine justice and retribution; personal devotion	Yes	Yes
Wisdom of Solomon	10 B.C. in Egypt	Wisdom personified; Jewish apologetic	Value of wisdom and faithfulness, immortality	Yes	Yes

ARCHAEOLOGICAL PERIODS OF PALESTINE

Archaeological Period	Approximate Dates *	Biblical Events
PALEOLITHIC (Old Stone Age)	Before 10,000 B.C.	Gen 1–11
MESOLITHIC (Middle Stone Age)	10,000–8000 B.C.	Gen 1–11
NEOLITHIC (New Stone Age)	8000–4500 B.C.	Gen 1–11
Pre-Pottery Neolithic	8000–6000 B.C.	
Pottery Neolithic	6000–4500 B.C.	
CHALCOLITHIC (Bronze/Stone Age)	4500–3150 B.C.	Gen 1–11
BRONZE (or CANAANITE)	3150–1200 B.C.	
Early Bronze	3150–2200 B.C.	Gen 1–11
I	3150–2850 B.C.	
II	2850–2650 B.C.	
III	2650–2350 B.C.	
IV	2350–2200 B.C.	
Middle Bronze	2200–1550 B.C.	
I	2200–1950 B.C.	Abraham
IIA	1950–1750 B.C.	Jacob enters Egypt
IIB	1750–1550 B.C.	
Late Bronze	1550–1200 B.C.	The exodus and conquest
I	1550–1400 B.C.	
IIA	1400–1300 B.C.	
IIB	1300–1200 B.C.	
IRON (or ISRAELITE)	1200–586 B.C.	
Iron I (or Early Iron)	1200–1000 B.C.	
IA	1200–1150 B.C.	
IB	1150–1000 B.C.	David becomes king
Iron II (or Middle Iron)	1000–800 B.C.	
IIA	1000–900 B.C.	
IIB	900–800 B.C.	
Iron III (or Iron IIC)	800–586 B.C.	Israel and Judah fall (722 and 586 B.C.)
PERSIAN (or BABYLONIAN/PERSIAN, or Late Iron)	586–332 B.C.	Babylonian captivity (586–539 B.C.)
HELLENISTIC	332–37 B.C.	
I	332–152 B.C.	
II (or Hasmonean/Maccabean)	152–37 B.C.	
ROMAN	37 B.C.–A.D. 324	
I (or Early Roman, or Herodian)	37 B.C.–A.D. 70	Jesus Christ
II (or Middle Roman)	A.D. 70–180	
III (or Late Roman)	A.D. 180–324	
BYZANTINE (Early Church Age of Roman Empire)	A.D. 324–640	
Early Byzantine	A.D. 324–491	
Late Byzantine	A.D. 491–640	

* Dates vary, but they give the reader some idea about the definition of the various archaeological time periods as they are utilized in current archaeological writings.

C
H
A
R
T
S

THE BIBLE IN ENGLISH
(Some translations are omitted due to space constraints)

OLD ENGLISH TRANSLATION (A.D. 300–1100)

A.D. 300s—First Christians arrived in Britain

A.D. 400s—Angles, Saxons, and Jutes arrive in Britain

A.D. 500–700—Evangelization of Angles, Saxons, and Jutes

A.D. 700–1100—Only parts of the Bible translated into "Old English"

MIDDLE ENGLISH TRANSLATION (1100–1500)

1066—Norman Invasion brings French influence into language development and creates "Middle English"

Important persons:

John Wycliffe—died 1384. Wanted to take gospel to the commoners. Began translating from Latin into English in 1380. Was assisted by:

Nicholas of Hereford—whose translation followed the Latin Vulgate very closely

AND

John Purvey—whose revision of Nicholas's translation used more idiomatic expressions.

Important events at the end of this period:

The Renaissance—a revival of learning occurred which prompted a renewed interest in the original Hebrew and Greek. A new challenge to authority also emerged.

The invention of the printing press (1453)—made printed material accessible to the masses rather than to a few.

The Protestant Reformation (beginning in 1517)—Martin Luther and those who followed had a tremendous desire to get the Bible into the hands of the common people.

MODERN ENGLISH TRANSLATION (1500–1900)

1525/6	William Tyndale translated New Testament into English from Greek. Was translating Old Testament at the time of his death as a martyr in 1536.
1535	Miles Coverdale completed and published first complete Bible in English from Tyndale's work, Greek and Hebrew, and other sources.
1537	**Matthew's Bible**. A complete English Bible from Tyndale's and Coverdale's work by John Rogers. Received royal sanction of King Henry VIII.
1539	**The Great Bible**. A revision by Coverdale of Matthew's Bible. Was placed in every church in England at the order of King Henry.
1560	**The Geneva Bible**. Produced by Protestant scholars in Geneva from the original languages and from Tyndale's work. (Sometimes called "Breeches Bible" because in Gen 3:7 Adam and Eve made "breeches" for themselves from fig leaves.)
1568	**The Bishop's Bible**. A revision of the Great Bible. Was authorized by the Church of England as their official translation.
1582 and 1609-10	**Rheims/Douai Translation**. Roman Catholic translation from the Latin Vulgate of the Old and New Testaments so named because of where they were translated: the Old Testament at Douai in 1609-10 preceded by the translation of the New Testament at Rheims in 1582.
1611	**The King James Version (or Authorized Version)**. Commissioned by King James I of England and translated by a number of Bible scholars. A revision of the 1602 edition of the Bishops' Bible with the aid of the Hebrew and Greek texts and a dependence upon the work of William Tyndale.
1885	**The Revised Version**. A revision of the Authorized Version incorporating more recently discovered manuscripts and more modern language usage. By a group of British scholars and some American scholars.

TWENTIETH-CENTURY ENGLISH TRANSLATIONS (1900–   )

1901   **The American Standard Version**. An American revision of the Authorized Version growing out of American scholars' participation in the Revised Version.

1903   **The New Testament in Modern Speech**. R. T. Weymouth's attempt to render Greek grammatical constructions carefully.

1924   **A New Translation of the Bible**. An idiomatic, colloquial, and sometimes Scottish translation by James Moffatt.

1927   **Centenary Translation of the New Testament**. Helen B. Montgomery's missionary heart produced a translation in the language of everyday life.

1937   **Williams New Testament**. By Charles B. Williams. A Baptist professor's attempt to translate into English the nuances of the Greek verbs.

1938   **The Bible: An American Translation**. E. J. Goodspeed and J. M. Powis Smith produced the first modern American translation with the Apocrypha.

1952   **The Revised Standard Version**. Revision of the American Standard Version and the King James Version by an international translation committee seeking to maintain literary awesomeness for worship.

1955   **The Holy Bible**. Translated by Ronald Knox, a Roman Catholic, from the Latin Vulgate.

1958   **The New Testament in Modern English**. A free translation by J. B. Phillips originally done for his youth club.

1965   **The Amplified Bible**. A version by the Lockman Foundation suggesting various wordings throughout the text.

1966   **The Jerusalem Bible**. Originally translated into French by Roman Catholic scholars from the original languages.

1969   **The New Berkeley (Modern Language) Bible**. A revision of the Berkeley Version of 1959 by Gerrit Verkuyl with attached notes.

1970   **The New English Bible**. A translation with literary quality but some idiosyncratic language. Translated by representatives of Britain's major churches and Bible societies and based on the most recent textual evidence.

1970   **The New American Bible**. A new translation by Roman Catholic scholars (the Bishops' Committee of the Confraternity of Christian Doctrine) from the original languages.

1971   **The New American Standard Bible**. A revision by the Lockman Foundation of the American Standard Version of 1901 with the goal of maintaining literal translation.

1971   **The Living Bible**. A conservative American paraphrase by Kenneth N. Taylor originally for his children (begun in 1962).

1976   **The Good News Bible (Today's English Version)**. A translation by the American Bible Society into "vernacular" English.

1979   **The New International Version**. A readable translation by evangelical scholars incorporating the most recent textual evidence.

1982   **The New King James Version**. A modernization of the King James Version of 1611. Based on the original language texts available to the King James Version translators.

1987   **The New Century Version**. A translation committee's update of the International Children's Bible.

1989   **The New Revised Standard Version**. A translation committee's update of the Revised Standard Version.

1989   **The Revised English Bible**. A British committee's update of the New English Bible maintaining literary quality but avoiding idiosyncratic language.

1991   **The Contemporary English Version (New Testament)**. A simplified text originally conceived for children and produced by the American Bible Society.

THE BOOKS OF THE BIBLE

39 Old Testament Books

Law | Poetry/Wisdom | Minor
History | Major Prophets | Prophets

Law
Genesis
Exodus
Leviticus
Numbers
Deuteronomy

History
Joshua
Judges
Ruth
1 Samuel
2 Samuel
1 Kings
2 Kings
1 Chronicles
2 Chronicles
Ezra
Nehemiah
Esther

Poetry/Wisdom
Job
Psalms
Proverbs
Ecclesiastes
Song of Solomon

Major Prophets
Isaiah
Jeremiah
Lamentations
Ezekiel
Daniel

Minor Prophets
Hosea
Joel
Amos
Obadiah
Jonah
Micah
Nahum
Habakkuk
Zephaniah
Haggai
Zechariah
Malachi

27 New Testament Books

Gospels | Letters of Paul | Prophecy
History | General Letters

Gospels
Matthew
Mark
Luke
John

History
Acts

Letters of Paul
Romans
1 Corinthians
2 Corinthians
Galatians
Ephesians
Philippians
Colossians
1 Thessalonians
2 Thessalonians
1 Timothy
2 Timothy
Titus
Philemon

General Letters
Hebrews
James
1 Peter
2 Peter
1 John
2 John
3 John
Jude

Prophecy
Revelation

COMPARISON OF LISTS OF THE OLD TESTAMENT BOOKS

RABBINIC CANON 24 BOOKS	SEPTUAGINT 53 BOOKS	ROMAN CATHOLIC OLD TESTAMENT 46 BOOKS
The Law	***Law***	***Law***
Genesis	Genesis	Genesis
Exodus	Exodus	Exodus
Leviticus	Leviticus	Leviticus
Numbers	Numbers	Numbers
Deuteronomy	Deuteronomy	Deuteronomy
The Prophets	***History***	***History***
The Former Prophets		
Joshua	Joshua	Joshua
Judges	Judges	Judges
1-2 Samuel	Ruth	Ruth
1-2 Kings	1 Kingdoms (1 Samuel)	1 Samuel (1 Kingdoms)
The Latter Prophets	2 Kingdoms (2 Samuel)	2 Samuel (2 Kingdoms)
Isaiah	3 Kingdoms (1 Kings)	1 Kings (3 Kingdoms)
Jeremiah	4 Kingdoms (2 Kings)	2 Kings (4 Kingdoms)
Ezekiel	1 Paralipomena (1 Chronicles)	1 Chronicles (1 Paralipomena)
The Twelve	2 Paralipomena (2 Chronicles)	2 Chronicles (2 Paralipomena)
Hosea	1 Esdras (Apocryphal Ezra)	Ezra (1 Esdras)
Joel	2 Esdras (Ezra-Nehemiah)	Nehemiah (2 Esdras)
Amos	Esther (with Apocryphal additions)	Tobit
Obadiah	Judith	Judith
Jonah	Tobit	Esther
Micah	1 Maccabees	1 Maccabees
Nahum	2 Maccabees	2 Maccabees
Habakkuk	3 Maccabees	
Zephaniah	4 Maccabees	
Haggai		***Poetry***
Zechariah	***Poetry***	Job
Malachi	Psalms	Psalms
	Odes (including the prayer of Manasseh)	Proverbs
The Writings	Proverbs	Ecclesiastes
Poetry	Ecclesiastes	Song of Songs
Psalms	Song of Songs	Wisdom of Solomon
Proverbs	Job	Ecclesiasticus (The Wisdom of
Job	Wisdom (of Solomon)	Jesus the son of Sirach)
Rolls—"the Festival Scrolls"	Sirach (Ecclesiasticus or The Wisdom	
Song of Songs	of Jesus the son of Sirach)	***Prophecy***
Ruth	Psalms of Solomon	Isaiah
Lamentations		Jeremiah
Ecclesiastes	***Prophecy***	Lamentations
Esther	The Twelve Prophets	Baruch (including the Letter
Others (History)	Hosea	of Jeremiah)
Daniel	Amos	Ezekiel
Ezra-Nehemiah	Micah	Daniel
1–2 Chronicles	Joel	Hosea
	Obadiah	Joel
	Jonah	Amos
	Nahum	Obadiah
	Habakkuk	Jonah
	Zephaniah	Micah
	Haggai	Nahum
	Zechariah	Habakkuk
	Malachi	Zephaniah
	Isaiah	Haggai
	Jeremiah	Zechariah
	Baruch	Malachi
	Lamentations	
	Letter of Jeremiah	***Appendix***
	Ezekiel	The Prayer of Manasseh
	Daniel (with apocryphal additions,	The two apocryphal books of
	including the Prayer of Azariah and	Esdras
	the Song of the Three Children,	
	Susanna, and Bel and the Dragon)	

The Canonical Books of the Old Testament ✱

▭ Books of Law

▭ Books of History

▭ Books of Poetry and Wisdom

▭ Books of the Major Prophets

▭ Books of the Minor Prophets

✱ Grouped according to the Christian canon

-21-

C H A R T S

DENOMINATIONAL PERSPECTIVES ON MAJOR DOCTRINES

	Baptist	Catholic	Church of Christ	Episcopal	Lutheran	Methodist	Pentecostal	Presbyterian
GOD	There is one and only one living and true God who reveals Himself to us as Father, Son, and Holy Spirit, with distinct personal attributes but without division of nature, essence, or being.	The one God is three by reason of three inner personal principles, Father, Son, (Word), and Holy Spirit. One God	Speaking where the Bible speaks and remaining silent where the Bible is silent, Churches of Christ prefer not to use the word "Trinity." While believing in Father, Son, and Holy Spirit, stress is on the Son, Jesus Christ.	"In unity of this God-head there be three persons of one substance, power, and eternity; the Father, the Son, and the Holy Ghost."	There is one Divine Essence, God; and yet there are three Persons of the same in substance, power and eternity. God is infinite in power, wisdom, and goodness. He is spirit and personal, creator and sustainer; and has revealed Himself as Father, Son, Spirit.	The three persons of the Godhead are "one in substance, power and eternity." God is infinite in three personalities: Father, Son, and Holy Spirit. All three are essential in revealing the one.	God is ultimate authority. The one true God has revealed Himself in three Persons: Father, Son, and Holy Spirit.	God made Himself known to us in three Persons: Father, Son, and Holy Spirit. The three Persons are one true, eternal God, the same in substance, equal in power and glory, though distinguished by personal properties.
HOLY SCRIPTURE	The Holy Bible was written by men divinely inspired and is the record of God's self-revelation to humanity. It has God for its author, salvation for its end, and truth without mixture of error for its matter.	The Bible teaches without error those truths which God wishes to reveal to all people for their eternal salvation. The church in her creeds summarizes basic doctrines of the Bible. Both Old and New Testaments and Apocrypha are believed divinely inspired.	Scripture is true, inspired, and completely sufficient for doctrine. Both Old and New Testaments are canonical, but the New Testament is primary since it reveals Christ.	The Word of God is the written record of God's self-revelation and of God's acts in history. Must be seen in the context of reason and tradition. Includes Old and New Testaments and Apocrypha.	The Scriptures are the Word of God, reliable, trustworthy, and understood through the Holy Spirit. Several confessional statements interpreting Scripture "participate in the normative authority of Scripture."	The Scriptures are the Word of God in Christ, the primary source and guideline for doctrine. Tradition, experience, and reason interact with Scripture in understanding God's Word.	The sixty-six books of the Bible contain all things necessary to salvation. The Bible is inspired by the Holy Spirit and is authoritative.	The Bible as the written revelation of God in Christ is the primary source of knowledge about God and His intentions for persons. As the inspired record of God's revelation, Scriptures contain instruction to salvation.
SALVATION	Salvation involves redemption of sinners who accept Jesus Christ as Lord and Savior. In its broadest sense, salvation includes regeneration, sanctification, and glorification.	Original sin interfered with God's plan for humanity. God sent His Son to save humanity from original sin and sins committed. Jesus saved humanity by His life and death and by rising from the dead and ascending into heaven. All who believe Jesus and are sorry for sins are saved.	All persons are sinful and need salvation but do not merit it. God offers salvation, and persons may decide to accept or reject it. Salvation comes through God's salvation through faith in Bible teachings and baptism. Apostasy is an option.	Redemption was wrought and wholeness of life is seen in the life, death, and resurrection of Jesus Christ. Individuals respond to God's salvation through baptism and spend a lifetime appropriating God's grace.	Salvation is God's gift offered to all people by the Holy Spirit through the preaching of God's Word.	Salvation comes by the grace of God upon a person's decision to say yes to God's gracious offer of salvation. Good works are a sign of salvation. Christians may renounce salvation (commit apostasy) or achieve a temporary state of holy perfection.	All persons need salvation to restore relationship with God because of sin. Salvation involves three stages including repentance and salvation, sanctification, and baptism of the Holy Spirit evidenced by speaking in tongues.	All persons are sinful and need salvation. We do not earn salvation; rather God elects some persons to salvation. These cannot refuse His offer (irresistible grace). God saves those who by faith repent and put their trust in Christ.

DENOMINATIONAL PERSPECTIVES ON MAJOR DOCTRINES

	Baptist	Catholic	Church of Christ	Episcopal	Lutheran	Methodist	Pentecostal	Presbyterian
BAPTISM	Christian baptism is the immersion of a believer in water in the name of the Father, Son, and Holy Spirit, symbolizing the believer's death to sin, burial of old life, and resurrection to new life in Christ.	Baptism is the sacrament of spiritual regeneration by which a person is incorporated into life with Christ and His church, given grace and cleansed from original and personal sin. It is administered by pouring water over the person, or the person is immersed in water.	Baptism is necessary for the remission of sins, to place one in Christ, and to place one in the church. The mode is immersion for believers only.	Baptism is the sacrament in which we say yes to God's prior act of grace toward us in Jesus Christ. Baptism is the preferred form, though pouring is often used. Both adults and infants are baptized.	Baptism plants the seed of salvation and may be administered by sprinkling. Other means of baptism using water and the Word of God are also accepted.	Baptism is a sacrament, a sign of God's grace by which He works within us to strengthen and confirm our faith. Infants are baptized as an initiation into Christian community by sprinkling, pouring, or immersion.	Baptism is a sacred ordinance to be obeyed, but it does not save. Believers are baptized by immersion.	A visible sign of God's word portraying Christ's redemption, baptism is administered by sprinkling or pouring water on adults. Baptism is the sign and seal of our ingrafting into Christ.
LORD'S SUPPER	The Lord's Supper is a symbolic act of obedience whereby members of the church, through partaking of the bread and fruit of the vine, memorialize the death of Christ and anticipate His second coming.	The Eucharist or mass is the central act of worship. The sacrament reenacts Christ's death and resurrection in ritual form. The actual body and blood of Christ are believed to be present in the elements (transubstantiation). Celebrated daily.	The Lord's Supper is an ordinance with a threefold meaning including: memorial meal commanded by Christ, proclamation of Christ's death for sins, and a time for examination of commitment to Christ. Observed only on Sunday at the church each week.	The Holy Eucharist is the sacrament commanded by Christ for the continual remembrance of His life, death, and resurrection until His coming again. The elements of bread and wine are received by those claiming Christ as Savior.	Holy Eucharist is one of three sacraments including baptism and absolution. Celebrated corporately, Eucharist is the Real Presence of the body and blood of Christ through sacramental union. When received in faith, grace through the Eucharist works forgiveness of sin, life, and salvation.	The Lord's Supper is a sign of love that Christians should share and a sacrament of our redemption by Christ's death. As a symbol the Lord's Supper represents Christ's work of atonement. As a sacrament the Spirit of God works through the bread and grape juice to call to mind Christ's death. Open to all Christians.	The Lord's Supper is a command of Christ to be obeyed in remembrance of Christ's death and sacrifice on the cross. The elements are symbolic of the spilled blood and the broken body. The supper is a time for individual examination and may be accompanied by foot washing.	The Lord's Supper is a sacrament in that the Spirit of God works in the believer who recalls Christ's work of redemption, reflects on his or commitment to Christ, and participates in the priesthood of believers by passing the bread and cup. The Lord is the host of the supper, and all who trust Him may partake.

THE HEBREW CANON OF THE OLD TESTAMENT

CLASSIFICATION OF THE BOOKS	HEBREW NAMES FOR THE BOOKS	ENGLISH NAMES FOR THE BOOKS
THE LAW (Torah)	In the beginning These are the names And He called In the wilderness These are the words	Genesis Exodus Leviticus Numbers Deuteronomy
FORMER PROPHETS	Joshua Judges 1 Samuel 2 Samuel 1 Kings 2 Kings	Joshua Judges 1 Samuel 2 Samuel 1 Kings 2 Kings
LATTER PROPHETS	Isaiah Jeremiah Ezekiel The Book of the Twelve (which includes) Hosea Joel Amos Obadiah Jonah Micah Nahum Habakkuk Zephaniah Haggai Zechariah Malachi	Isaiah Jeremiah Ezekiel Hosea Joel Amos Obadiah Jonah Micah Nahum Habakkuk Zephaniah Haggai Zechariah Malachi
THE WRITINGS (HAGIOGRAPHA)	Praises Job Proverbs Ruth Song of Songs The Preacher How! Esther Daniel Ezra / / Nehemiah 1 The words of the days 2 The words of the days	Psalms Job Proverbs Ruth Song of Solomon Ecclesiastes Lamentations Esther Daniel Ezra Nehemiah 1 Chronicles 2 Chronicles

NAMES OF GOD

NAME	REFERENCE	MEANING	NIV EQUIVALENT
HEBREW NAMES			
Adonai	Ps 2:4	Lord, Master	Lord
El -Berith	Judg 9:46	God of the Covenant	El -Berith
El Elyon	Gen 14:18-20	Most High God/ Exalted One	God Most High
El Olam	Gen 21:33	The Eternal God	The Eternal God
El Shaddai	Gen 17:1-2	All Powerful God	God Almighty
Qedosh Yisra'el	Isa 1:4	The Holy One of Israel	The Holy One of Israel
Shapat	Gen 18:25	Judge/Ruler	Judge
Yahweh-jereh	Gen 22:14	Yahweh Provides	The LORD Will Provide
Yahweh-seba'ot	1 Sam 1:3	Yahweh of Armies	LORD Almighty
Yahweh-shalom	Judg 6:24	Yahweh Is Peace	The LORD Is Peace
Yahweh-tsidkenu	Jer 23:6	Yahweh Our Righteousness	The LORD Our Righteousness
ARAMAIC NAMES			
Attiq yomin	Dan 7:9	Ancient of Days	Ancient of Days
Illaya	Dan 7:25	Most High	Most High

C H A R T S

NEW TESTAMENT APOCRYPHA

TYPE	TITLE	CONTENT	PURPOSE	DATE OF COMPOSITION
INFANCY GOSPELS	Protoevangelium of James	Miracles connected with Mary	Glorify Mary	150
	Infancy Gospel of Thomas	Miracles of Jesus as child	Fill in silent years of Jesus' life	200
PASSION GOSPELS	Gospel of Peter	Crucifixion and resurrection unconnected to Jewish history and without notes of salvation through the cross	Prove resurrection; put guilt on Jews; down-play Christ's humanity; emphasize miracles	150
	Gospel of Nicodemus (Acts of Pilate)	Dating of crucifixion; testimonies to innocence of Jesus and of Mary; resurrection appearances; guilt of Jews; Jesus' descent into hell	Prove Jesus innocent and Jews guilty; prove resurrection	150?
JEWISH CHRISTIAN GOSPELS	Gospel of Nazareans	Editing of Matthew; with some expansions	Uncertain; some ethical motivations	135
	Gospel of Ebionites	Abbreviation of Synoptic Gospels; at times Jesus narrates story.	Oppose virgin birth; emphasize union of Christ and Spirit at baptism; oppose temple sacrifice	150
	Gospel of Hebrews	Resurrection appearance to James; James at last supper; Holy Spirit is female; Spirit rests in and unites with Jesus.	Lift position of James; support mystical piety	150
HERETICAL GOSPELS	Gospel of Truth	Homily on Jesus without narrative of His life or sayings	Define gospel in Gnostic terms	160
	Gospel of Thomas	114 secret sayings of Jesus	Gnostic teachings	200
APOCRYPHAL ACTS	Acts of John	Life of John with journey to Rome, life on Patmos, death in Ephesus; teachings of John	Gnostic teaching	225
	Acts of Peter	Disputes between Peter and Simon in Jerusalem and Rome; miracles; Peter's death	God's victory over Satan; information about Peter; moral teachings	185
	Acts of Paul	Acts of Paul and Thecla, correspondence with Corinthians; further missionary work; miracles; martyrdom	Support Paul's image; build up the church; teach sexual continence; hope of resurrection	190
	Acts of Andrew	Journey across Asia Minor into Greece; miracles; martyrdom	Self-knowledge; deny material world; fight Satan	150
	Acts of Thomas	Journeys; miracles; hymns; anointings; Eucharist; conversions; martyrdom	Gnostic salvation doctrine; asceticism; no baptism	215
APOCRYPHAL EPISTLES	Proclamation of Peter	Summary of apostolic gospel	Apology for Christianity	100
	Epistle to Laodiceans	Combination of Pauline passages based on Col 4:16	Supply lost letter of Paul	300?
APOCRYPHAL APOCALYPSES	Ascension of Isaiah	Martyrdom; heavenly journey	Supply prophecy of Christ	225?
	Apocalypse of Peter	Vision of heaven and of hell	Provide explicit teaching on afterlife	135

PRAYERS OF THE BIBLE

Type of Prayer	Meaning	Old Testament Example	New Testament Example	Jesus' Teaching
Confession	Acknowledging sin and helplessness and seeking God's mercy	Ps 51	Luke 18:13	Luke 15:11-24; Luke 18:10-24
Praise	Adoring God for who He is	1 Chr 29:10-13	Luke 1:46-55	Matt 6:9
Thanksgiving	Expressing gratitude to God for what He has done	Ps 105:1-7	1 Thess 5:16-18	Luke 17:11-19
Petition	Making personal request of God	Gen 24:12-14	Acts 1:24-26	Matt 7:7-12
Intercession	Making request of God on behalf of another	Exod 32:11-13, 31-32	Phil 1:9-11	John 17:9,20-21
Commitment	Expressing loyalty to God and His work	1 Kgs 8:56-61	Acts 4:24-30	Matt 6:10; Mark 14:32-42; Luke 6:46-49
Forgiveness	Seeking mercy for personal sin or the sin of others	Dan 9:4-19	Acts 7:60	Matt 6:12,14-15; Luke 6:27-36; 23:33-34
Confidence	Affirming God's all-sufficiency and the believer's security in His love	Ps 23	Luke 2:29-32	Matt 6:5-15; 7:11; John 11:41-42
Benediction	A request for God's blessing	Num 6:24-26	Jude 24-25	Luke 24:50-51

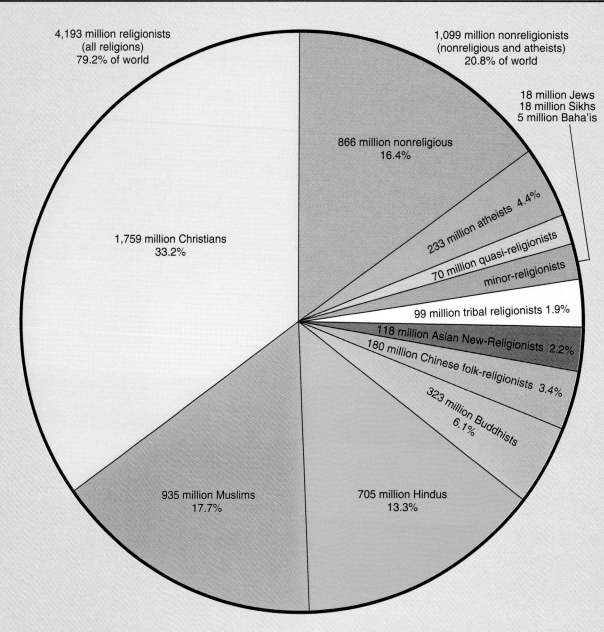

RELIGIONS OF THE WORLD*

4,193 million religionists
(all religions)
79.2% of world

1,099 million nonreligionists
(nonreligious and atheists)
20.8% of world

18 million Jews
18 million Sikhs
5 million Baha'is

866 million nonreligious
16.4%

1,759 million Christians
33.2%

233 million atheists 4.4%

70 million quasi-religionists

minor-religionists

99 million tribal religionists 1.9%

118 million Asian New-Religionists 2.2%

180 million Chinese folk-religionists 3.4%

323 million Buddhists
6.1%

935 million Muslims
17.7%

705 million Hindus
13.3%

RELIGION (30,000 religions, analyzable into 33 major religious and antireligious blocs)

ADHERENCE TO RELIGION IN 1990
4,193 million religionists (all religions) (annual increase 1.9% p.a.)
   2,000 million popular-religionists
     430 million New Age/occult/neo-Hindu cultists
     720 million Christian popular-religionist-pietists
     70 million quasi-religionists, including 6.9 million
       Freemasons (males)
1,099 million nonreligionists (2.8% p.a.)
   866 million nonreligious (2.8% p.a.)
   233 million atheists (1.7% p.a.)

ADHERENTS OF NON-CHRISTIAN RELIGIONS
2,434 million non-Christian religionists (annual increase 2.3% p.a.)

GREAT WORLD RELIGIONS
935 million Muslims (2.7% p.a.)
   780 million Sunnis (2.7% p.a.)
   145 million Shias (Shiites) (2.9% p.a.)
    18 million Ismailis (3.4% p.a.)
    10 million Ahmadis (4.2% p.a.)
705 million Hindus (2.3% p.a.)
   493 million Vaishnavites (2.3% p.a.)
   175 million Shaivites (2.3% p.a.)

   20 million Saktists (2.2% p.a.)
   12 million Neo-Hindus (3.3% p.a.)
    4 million Reformed Hindus (2.5% p.a.)
323 million Buddhists (1.7% p.a.)
   182 million Mahayana (1.7% p.a.)
   122 million Theravada (1.7% p.a.)
    19 million Tantrayana (Lamaists) (1.7% p.a.)

OTHER MAJOR RELIGIONS
180 million Chinese folk-religionists (0.8% p.a.)
118 million Asian New-Religionists (2.3% p.a.)
  99 million tribal religionists (0.2% p.a.)

MINOR RELIGIONS
18 million Jews (1.1% p.a.)
18 million Sikhs (2.9% p.a.)
  8 million non-Christian Spiritists (5.5% p.a.)
  5 million Baha'is (3.6% p.a.)
  3 million Shintoists (-1.7% p.a.)
  3 million Jains (2.0% p.a.)

CHRISTIANS AND NON-CHRISTIANS
1,759 million Christians (2.2% p.a.)
3,533 million non-Christians (1.7% p.a.)

✱ All data as of mid 1990

STAGES IN THE DEVELOPMENT OF THE NEW TESTAMENT CANON

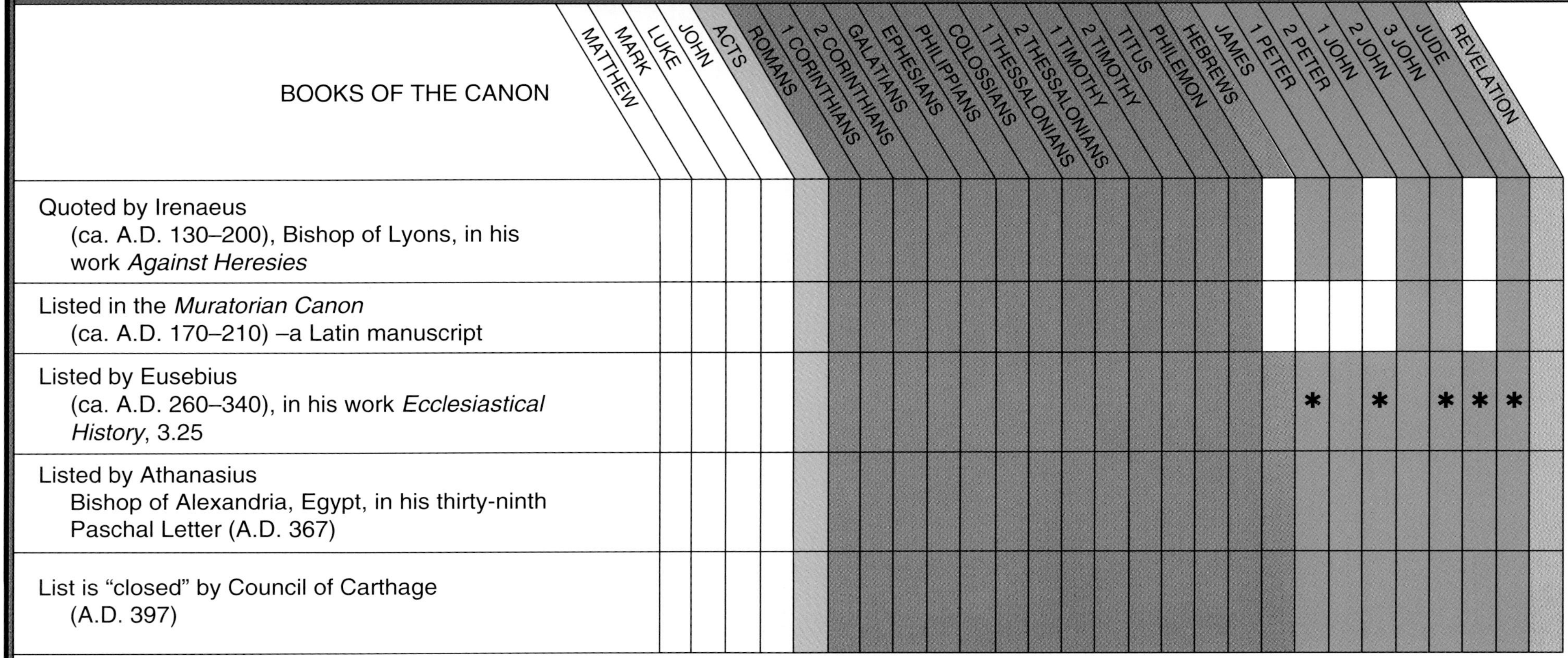

BOOKS OF THE CANON	Quoted by Irenaeus (ca. A.D. 130–200), Bishop of Lyons, in his work *Against Heresies*	Listed in the *Muratorian Canon* (ca. A.D. 170–210) –a Latin manuscript	Listed by Eusebius (ca. A.D. 260–340), in his work *Ecclesiastical History*, 3.25	Listed by Athanasius Bishop of Alexandria, Egypt, in his thirty-ninth Paschal Letter (A.D. 367)	List is "closed" by Council of Carthage (A.D. 397)
MATTHEW					
MARK					
LUKE					
JOHN					
ACTS					
ROMANS					
1 CORINTHIANS					
2 CORINTHIANS					
GALATIANS					
EPHESIANS					
PHILIPPIANS					
COLOSSIANS					
1 THESSALONIANS					
2 THESSALONIANS					
1 TIMOTHY					
2 TIMOTHY					
TITUS					
PHILEMON					
HEBREWS					
JAMES			*		
1 PETER					
2 PETER			*		
1 JOHN					
2 JOHN			*		
3 JOHN			*		
JUDE			*		
REVELATION			*		

* "Disputed Books" (not yet universally accepted)—according to Eusebius

Legend (shading):
- GOSPELS
- BOOK OF HISTORY OF THE EARLY CHURCH
- LETTERS OF PAUL (probably collected before the end of the first century)
- LETTER BY UNKNOWN AUTHOR
- GENERAL, OR "CATHOLIC," LETTERS
- BOOK OF PROPHECY

-30-

TABLE OF WEIGHTS AND MEASURES

WEIGHT

Biblical Unit	Language	Biblical Measure	U.S. Equivalent	Metric Equivalent	Various Translations
Gerah	Hebrew	1/20 shekel	1/50 ounce	.6 gram	gerah; oboli
Bekah	Hebrew	1/2 shekel or 10 gerahs	1/5 ounce	5.7 grams	bekah; half a shekel; quarter ounce; fifty cents
Pim	Hebrew	2/3 shekel	1/3 ounce	7.6 grams	2/3 of a shekel; quarter
Shekel	Hebrew	2 bekahs	2/5 ounce	11.5 grams	shekel; piece; dollar; fifty dollars
Litra (Pound)	Greco-Roman	30 shekels	12 ounces	.4 kilogram	pound; pounds
Mina	Hebrew/Greek	50 shekels	1 1/4 pounds	.6 kilogram	mina; pound
Talent	Hebrew/Greek	3000 shekels or 60 minas	75 pounds/ 88 pounds	34 kilograms/ 40 kilograms	talents/talent; 100 pounds

LENGTH

Biblical Unit	Language	Biblical Measure	U.S. Equivalent	Metric Equivalent	Various Translations
Handbreadth	Hebrew	1/6 cubit or 1/3 span	3 inches	8 centimeters	handbreadth; three inches; four inches
Span	Hebrew	1/2 cubit or 3 handbreadths	9 inches	23 centimeters	span
Cubit/Pechys	Hebrew/Greek	2 spans	18 inches	.5 meter	cubit(s); yard; half a yard; foot
Fathom	Greco-Roman	4 cubits	2 yards	2 meters	fathom; six feet
Kalamos	Greco-Roman	6 cubits	3 yards	3 meters	rod; reed; measuring rod
Stadion	Greco-Roman	1/8 milion or 400 cubits	1/8 mile	185 meters	miles; furlongs; race
Milion	Greco-Roman	8 stadia	1,620 yards	1.5 kilometer	mile

DRY MEASURE

Biblical Unit	Language	Biblical Measure	U.S. Equivalent	Metric Equivalent	Various Translations
Xestēs	Greco-Roman	1/2 cab	1 1/6 pints	.5 liter	pots; pitchers; kettles; copper pots; copper bowls; vessels of bronze
Cab	Hebrew	1/18 ephah	1 quart	1 liter	cab; kab
Choinix	Greco-Roman	1/18 ephah	1 quart	1 liter	measure; quart
Omer	Hebrew	1/10 ephah	2 quarts	2 liters	omer; tenth of a deal; tenth of an ephah; six pints
Seah/Saton	Hebrew/Greek	1/3 ephah	7 quarts	7.3 liters	measures; pecks; large amounts
Modios	Greco-Roman	4 omers	1 peck or 1/4 bushel	9 liters	bushel; bowl; peck-measure corn-measure; meal-tub
Ephah [Bath]	Hebrew	10 omers	3/5 bushel	22 liters	bushel; peck; deal; part; measure; six pints; seven pints
Lethek	Hebrew	5 ephahs	3 bushels	110 liters	half homer; half sack
Cor [Homer]/Koros	Hebrew/Greek	10 ephahs	6 bushels or 200 quarts/ 14.9 bushels or 500 quarts	220 liters/ 525 liters	cor; homer; sack; measures; bushels/sacks; measures; bushels; containers

LIQUID MEASURE

Biblical Unit	Language	Biblical Measure	U.S. Equivalent	Metric Equivalent	Various Translations
Log	Hebrew	1/72 bath	1/3 quart	.3 liter	log; pint; cotulus
Xestēs	Greco-Roman	1/8 hin	1 1/6 pints	.5 liter	pots; pitchers; kettles; copper pots; copper bowls; vessels of bronze
Hin	Hebrew	1/6 bath	1 gallon or 4 quarts	4 liters	hin; pints
Bath/Batos [Ephah]	Hebrew/Greek	6 hins	6 gallons	22 liters	gallon(s); barrels; liquid measure/ gallons; barrels; measures
Metretes	Greco-Roman	10 hins	10 gallons	39 liters	firkins; gallons
Cor [Homer]/Koros	Hebrew/Greek	10 baths	60 gallons	220 liters	cor; homer; sack; measures; bushels/sacks; measures; bushels; containers

TIME LINE

Pentateuch

BIBLICAL HISTORY

| CREATION, FALL, FLOOD, BABEL | PATRIARCHS |

2100   2000   1900   1800

Earlier
Dating
System

Isaac   Joseph

Abraham   Jacob

| Undatable Past - Creation, Fall, Flood, Babel | PATRIARCHS | EGYPTIAN SLAVERY |

2100   2000   1900   1800

Later
Dating
System

ANCIENT HISTORY

WORLD HISTORY

| EARLY BRONZE AGE | MIDDLE BRONZE AGE |

2500   2400   2300   2200   2100   2000   1900   1800

Earliest
Papyrus

Hammurabi

—Sumerian Age——————   —Empire of Akkad—   —Ur—   —Babylonian—
                                                                Dynasty

—Egyptian Old Kingdom————————————   —Egyptian Intermediate Kingdoms—
  Pyramids

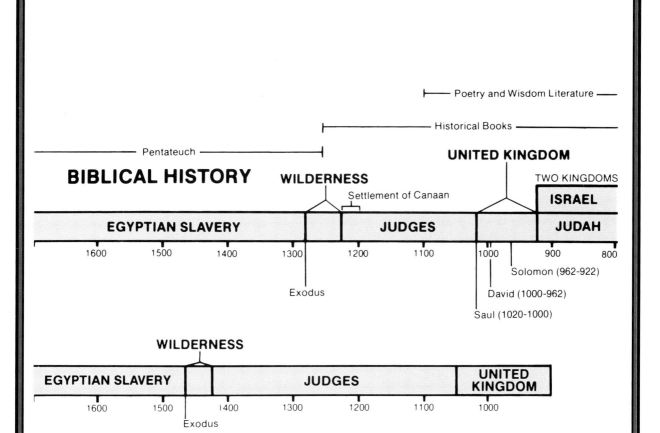

BIBLICAL HISTORY

├── Poetry and Wisdom Literature ──┤

├──────── Historical Books ────────┤

├── Pentateuch ──┤

WILDERNESS

UNITED KINGDOM

TWO KINGDOMS

Settlement of Canaan

ISRAEL

| EGYPTIAN SLAVERY | | JUDGES | | JUDAH |

1600   1500   1400   1300   1200   1100   1000   900   800

Exodus

Solomon (962-922)

David (1000-962)

Saul (1020-1000)

WILDERNESS

| EGYPTIAN SLAVERY | | JUDGES | UNITED KINGDOM |

1600   1500   i400   1300   1200   1100   1000

Exodus

-33-

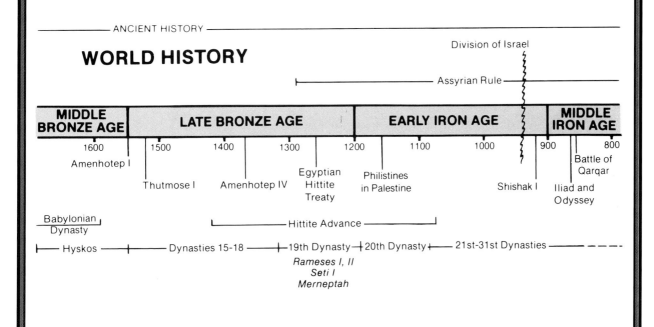

├────── ANCIENT HISTORY ──────┤

WORLD HISTORY

Division of Israel

├──── Assyrian Rule ────┤

| MIDDLE BRONZE AGE | LATE BRONZE AGE | EARLY IRON AGE | MIDDLE IRON AGE |

1600   1500   1400   1300   1200   1100   1000   900   800

Amenhotep I

Thutmose I

Amenhotep IV

Egyptian Hittite Treaty

Philistines in Palestine

Shishak I

Battle of Qarqar

Iliad and Odyssey

Babylonian Dynasty

├── Hittite Advance ──┤

├── Hyskos ──┤── Dynasties 15-18 ──┤ 19th Dynasty ┤ 20th Dynasty ├── 21st-31st Dynasties ── ── ──

Rameses I, II
Seti I
Merneptah

The Prophets

Poetry and Wisdom Literature

Historical Books

BIBLICAL HISTORY

TWO KINGDOMS

ISRAEL

Fall of Jerusalem

RESTORATION

JUDAH   **EXILE**   **INTERBIBLICAL PERIOD**

700   600   500   400   300   200   100   0

Fall of
Samaria

Joel

Dedication
of Second
Temple

Malachi
Nehemiah

Ezra

Ezekiel

Haggai
Zechariah

Daniel

PRE-EXILE PROPHETS

850   788   725 / 665   600

Elijah   Elisha   Jonah

Micah

Isaiah

Habakkuk

Hosea

Zephaniah
Jeremiah
Nahum

Amos

Old Testament Canonization Process

400   200   100   0   300   100

Judaism's
Bible
"Torah"
(Law)

Canonization
of the
"Nebi'im"
(Prophets)

"Kethubim"
(Writings)
established
but not fixed

Rabbinic
Discussions
at Jamnia
fix Hebrew
Canon

ANCIENT HISTORY

WORLD HISTORY

Babylonian
Rule

Persian
Rule

Ptolemies
(Egypt)

Selucid Kings
(Syrian)

MIDDLE IRON AGE   **LATE IRON AGE**   **HELLENISTIC PERIOD**

700   600   500   400   300   200   100

Nebuchadnezzar II

Plato

Stoicism

Qumran
Community

Sennacherib

Neco II

Socrates

Alexander
The Great

Cleopatra

Sargon II

Xerxes

Epicurus

Tiglath-Pileser III   Fall of
Nineveh

Darius I

Aristotle

Cyrus

End of Egyptian Dynasties

-34-

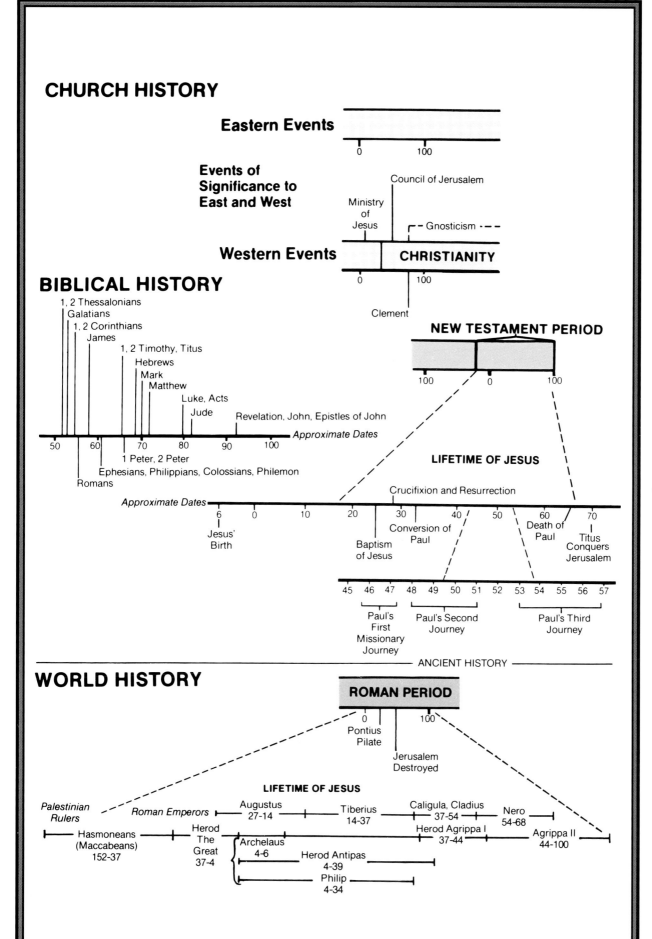

CHURCH HISTORY

Eastern Events

0   100

Events of
Significance to
East and West

Council of Jerusalem

Ministry
of
Jesus

─ Gnosticism ─ ─ ─

Western Events   **CHRISTIANITY**

0   100

Clement

BIBLICAL HISTORY

1, 2 Thessalonians
Galatians
1, 2 Corinthians
James
1, 2 Timothy, Titus
Hebrews
Mark
Matthew
Luke, Acts
Jude
Revelation, John, Epistles of John
Approximate Dates

50   60   70   80   90   100

1 Peter, 2 Peter
Ephesians, Philippians, Colossians, Philemon
Romans

NEW TESTAMENT PERIOD

100   0   100

LIFETIME OF JESUS

Crucifixion and Resurrection

Approximate Dates

6   0   10   20   30   40   50   60   70

Jesus'
Birth

Conversion of
Paul

Baptism
of Jesus

Death of
Paul

Titus
Conquers
Jerusalem

45 46 47 48 49 50 51 52 53 54 55 56 57

Paul's
First
Missionary
Journey

Paul's Second
Journey

Paul's Third
Journey

─────── ANCIENT HISTORY ───────

WORLD HISTORY

ROMAN PERIOD

0   100

Pontius
Pilate

Jerusalem
Destroyed

LIFETIME OF JESUS

*Palestinian
Rulers*

Roman Emperors

Augustus
27-14

Tiberius
14-37

Caligula, Cladius
37-54

Nero
54-68

Hasmoneans
(Maccabeans)
152-37

Herod
The
Great
37-4

Archelaus
4-6

Herod Antipas
4-39

Philip
4-34

Herod Agrippa I
37-44

Agrippa II
44-100

CHURCH HISTORY

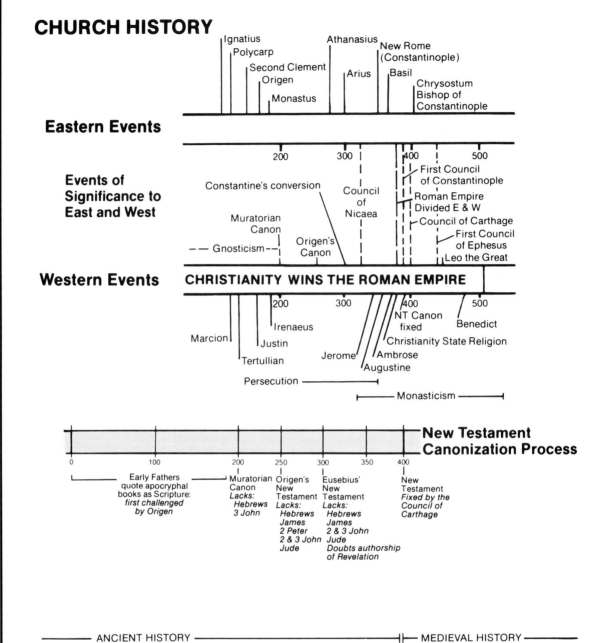

Eastern Events

Ignatius
Polycarp
Second Clement
Origen
Monastus
Athanasius
Arius
New Rome
(Constantinople)
Basil
Chrysostum
Bishop of
Constantinople

200   300   400   500

**Events of
Significance to
East and West**

Constantine's conversion
Council
of
Nicaea
First Council
of Constantinople
Roman Empire
Divided E & W
Council of Carthage
First Council
of Ephesus
Leo the Great

Muratorian
Canon
— — Gnosticism — —
Origen's
Canon

Western Events   **CHRISTIANITY WINS THE ROMAN EMPIRE**

200   300   400   500

Marcion
Justin
Tertullian
Irenaeus
Jerome
Augustine
Ambrose
NT Canon
fixed
Christianity State Religion
Benedict

Persecution ——————

|—— Monasticism ——|

**New Testament
Canonization Process**

0   100   200   250   300   350   400

Early Fathers
quote apocryphal
books as Scripture:
*first challenged
by Origen*

Muratorian
Canon
*Lacks:
Hebrews
3 John*

Origen's
New
Testament
*Lacks:
Hebrews
James
2 Peter
2 & 3 John
Jude*

Eusebius'
New
Testament
*Lacks:
Hebrews
James
2 & 3 John
Jude
Doubts authorship
of Revelation*

New
Testament
*Fixed by the
Council of
Carthage*

——— ANCIENT HISTORY ——————————————|—|— MEDIEVAL HISTORY ———

WORLD HISTORY

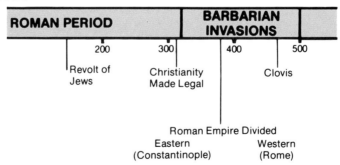

ROMAN PERIOD   **BARBARIAN
INVASIONS**

200   300   400   500

Revolt of
Jews
Christianity
Made Legal
Clovis

Roman Empire Divided
Eastern
(Constantinople)
Western
(Rome)

CHURCH HISTORY

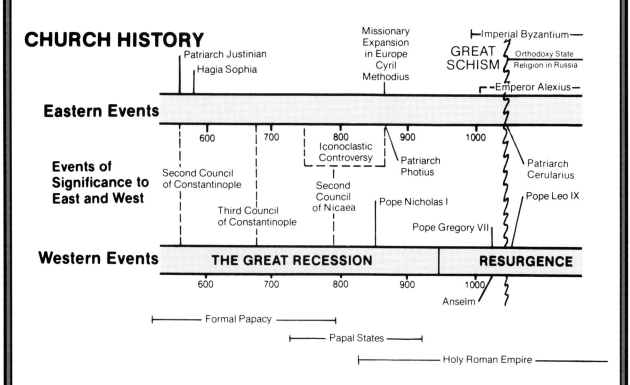

Patriarch Justinian
Hagia Sophia

Missionary
Expansion
in Europe
Cyril
Methodius

Imperial Byzantium

GREAT
SCHISM

Orthodoxy State
Religion in Russia

Emperor Alexius

Eastern Events

600   700   800
Iconoclastic
Controversy   900   1000

**Events of
Significance to
East and West**

Second Council
of Constantinople

Third Council
of Constantinople

Second
Council
of Nicaea

Patriarch
Photius

Pope Nicholas I

Pope Gregory VII

Patriarch
Cerularius

Pope Leo IX

Western Events | THE GREAT RECESSION | RESURGENCE

600   700   800   900   1000

Anselm

Formal Papacy

Papal States

Holy Roman Empire

Doctrines Addressed by the Early Church Councils

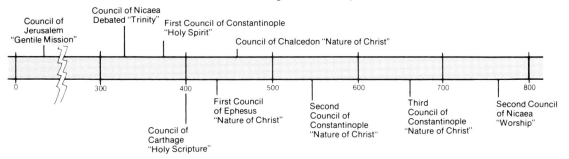

Council of
Jerusalem
"Gentile Mission"

Council of Nicaea
Debated "Trinity"

First Council of Constantinople
"Holy Spirit"

Council of Chalcedon "Nature of Christ"

0   300   400   500   600   700   800

Council of
Carthage
"Holy Scripture"

First Council
of Ephesus
"Nature of Christ"

Second
Council of
Constantinople
"Nature of Christ"

Third
Council of
Constantinople
"Nature of Christ"

Second Council
of Nicaea
"Worship"

MEDIEVAL HISTORY

WORLD HISTORY

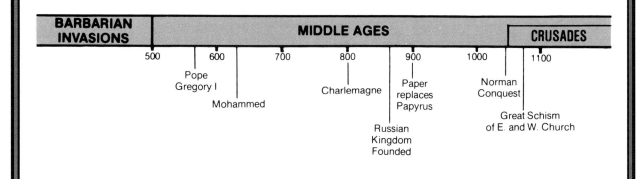

BARBARIAN
INVASIONS | MIDDLE AGES | CRUSADES

500   600   700   800   900   1000   1100

Pope
Gregory I

Mohammed

Charlemagne

Paper
replaces
Papyrus

Russian
Kingdom
Founded

Norman
Conquest

Great Schism
of E. and W. Church

-37-

C
H
A
R
T
S

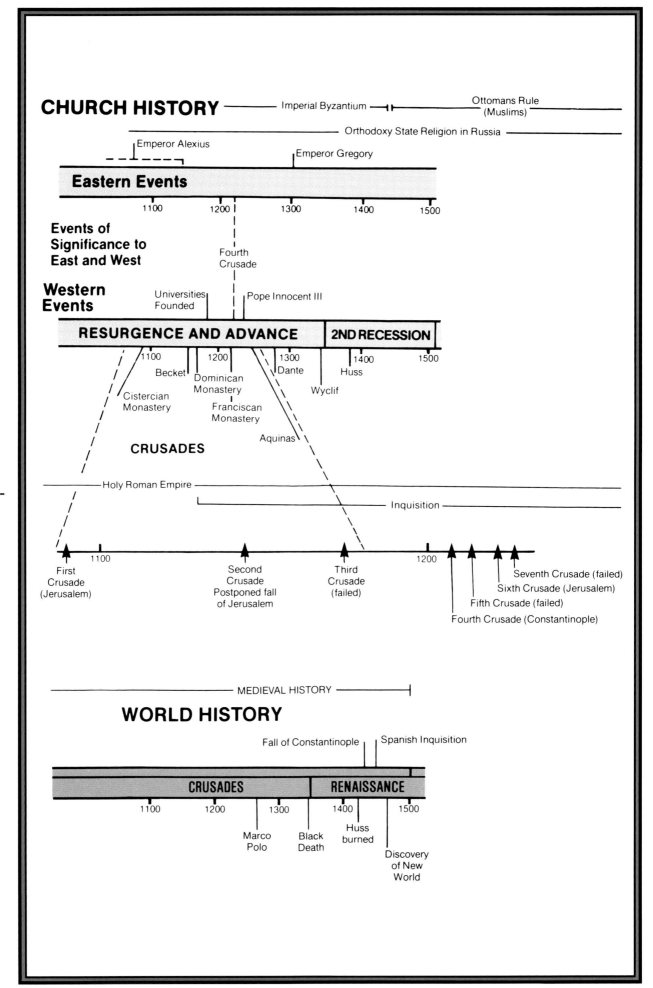

CHURCH HISTORY ———— Imperial Byzantium ——|—| Ottomans Rule (Muslims)

———————————— Orthodoxy State Religion in Russia ————————

Emperor Alexius   Emperor Gregory

Eastern Events

1100   1200   1300   1400   1500

**Events of
Significance to
East and West**

Fourth
Crusade

**Western
Events**

Universities   Pope Innocent III
Founded

RESURGENCE AND ADVANCE   2ND RECESSION

1100   1200   1300   1400   1500

Becket   Dante   Huss

Cistercian   Dominican   Wyclif
Monastery   Monastery

Franciscan
Monastery

Aquinas

CRUSADES

———— Holy Roman Empire ————————————————

———————— Inquisition ————————

First   Second   Third   Seventh Crusade (failed)
Crusade   Crusade   Crusade   Sixth Crusade (Jerusalem)
(Jerusalem)   Postponed fall (failed)   Fifth Crusade (failed)
               of Jerusalem   Fourth Crusade (Constantinople)

1100   1200

———————— MEDIEVAL HISTORY ————————|

WORLD HISTORY

Fall of Constantinople   Spanish Inquisition

CRUSADES   RENAISSANCE

1100   1200   1300   1400   1500

Marco   Black   Huss
Polo   Death   burned

                        Discovery
                        of New
                        World

-38-

CHURCH HISTORY

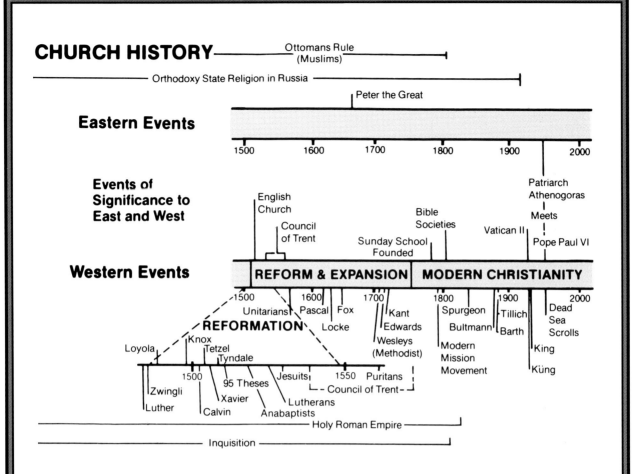

Ottomans Rule (Muslims)

Orthodoxy State Religion in Russia

Peter the Great

Eastern Events

1500 1600 1700 1800 1900 2000

Events of Significance to East and West

English Church
Council of Trent
Bible Societies
Sunday School Founded
Vatican II
Patriarch Athenogoras Meets
Pope Paul VI

Western Events

REFORM & EXPANSION   MODERN CHRISTIANITY

1500 1600 1700 1800 1900 2000

REFORMATION
Unitarians Pascal Fox Kant
Locke Edwards
Wesleys (Methodist)
Spurgeon Tillich Dead Sea Scrolls
Bultmann Barth
Modern Mission Movement King Küng

Loyola Knox Tetzel Tyndale
1500 1550 Puritans
Zwingli 95 Theses Jesuits Council of Trent
Luther Xavier Lutherans
Calvin Anabaptists

Holy Roman Empire

Inquisition

-39-

WORLD HISTORY

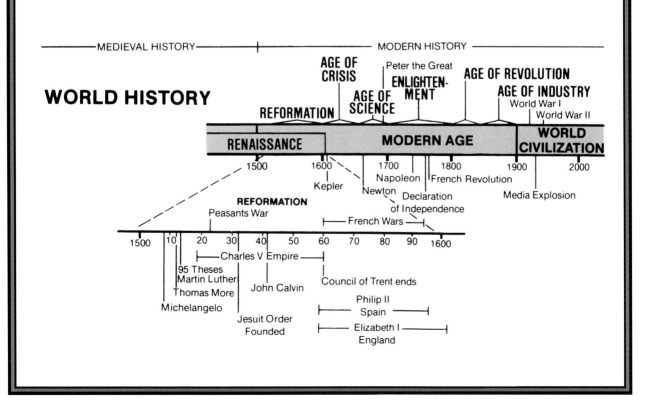

MEDIEVAL HISTORY   MODERN HISTORY

AGE OF CRISIS
Peter the Great
AGE OF SCIENCE
ENLIGHTEN-MENT
AGE OF REVOLUTION
AGE OF INDUSTRY
REFORMATION
World War I
World War II

RENAISSANCE   MODERN AGE   WORLD CIVILIZATION

1500 1600 1700 1800 1900 2000
Kepler Napoleon French Revolution
Newton Declaration of Independence Media Explosion

REFORMATION
Peasants War
French Wars

1500 10 20 30 40 50 60 70 80 90 1600
Charles V Empire
95 Theses
Martin Luther
Thomas More
John Calvin
Council of Trent ends
Michelangelo
Philip II Spain
Jesuit Order Founded
Elizabeth I England

OLD TESTAMENT CHARTS

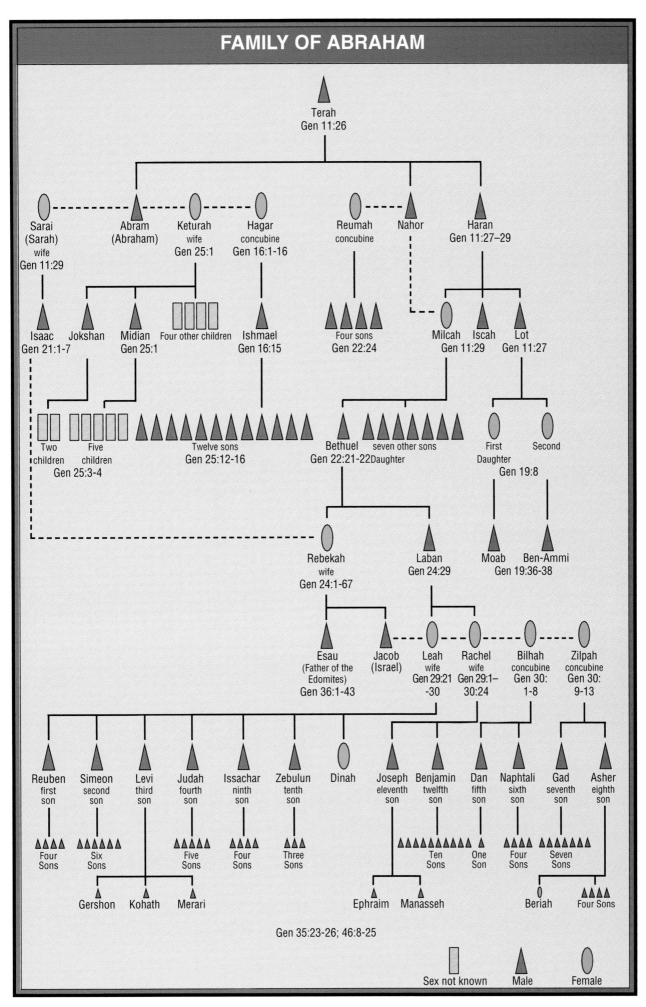

FAMILY OF ABRAHAM

Terah
Gen 11:26

Sarai (Sarah)
wife
Gen 11:29

Abram (Abraham)

Keturah
wife
Gen 25:1

Hagar
concubine
Gen 16:1-16

Reumah
concubine

Nahor

Haran
Gen 11:27–29

Isaac
Gen 21:1-7

Jokshan

Midian
Gen 25:1

Four other children

Ishmael
Gen 16:15

Four sons
Gen 22:24

Milcah
Gen 11:29

Iscah

Lot
Gen 11:27

Two children

Five children
Gen 25:3-4

Twelve sons
Gen 25:12-16

Bethuel
Gen 22:21-22

seven other sons

Daughter

First Daughter

Second Daughter
Gen 19:8

Rebekah
wife
Gen 24:1-67

Laban
Gen 24:29

Moab

Ben-Ammi
Gen 19:36-38

Esau
(Father of the Edomites)
Gen 36:1-43

Jacob
(Israel)

Leah
wife
Gen 29:21-30

Rachel
wife
Gen 29:1–30:24

Bilhah
concubine
Gen 30:1-8

Zilpah
concubine
Gen 30:9-13

Reuben
first
son

Simeon
second
son

Levi
third
son

Judah
fourth
son

Issachar
ninth
son

Zebulun
tenth
son

Dinah

Joseph
eleventh
son

Benjamin
twelfth
son

Dan
fifth
son

Naphtali
sixth
son

Gad
seventh
son

Asher
eighth
son

Four Sons

Six Sons

Five Sons

Four Sons

Three Sons

Ten Sons

One Son

Four Sons

Seven Sons

Gershon   Kohath   Merari

Ephraim   Manasseh

Beriah   Four Sons

Gen 35:23-26; 46:8-25

Sex not known   Male   Female

-43-

ASSYRIAN RULERS

RULER	DATES OF RULE	SCRIPTURE REFERENCE
Ashur-uballit I	1354–1318 B.C.	
Adad-nirari I	1318–1264 B.C.	
Shalmaneser I (Shulman-asharid)	1264–1234 B.C.	
Tukulti-Ninurta I	1234–1197 B.C.	
Ashur-dan I	1179–1133 B.C.	
Tiglath-pileser I (Tukulti-apil-Ešarra)	1115–1076 B.C.	
Ashur-rabi II	1012–972 B.C.	
Ashur-resh-ishi II	972–967 B.C.	
Tiglath-pileser II	967–935 B.C.	
Ashur-dan II	935–912 B.C.	
Adad-nirari II	912–889 B.C.	
Tukulti-Ninurta II	889–884 B.C.	
Ashurnasirpal II (Ashur-nasir-apli II)	884–858 B.C.	
Shalmaneser III (Shalman-Ashar-id II)	858–824 B.C.	
Shamsi-Adad V	824–810 B.C.	
Adad-nirari III	810–782 B.C.	
Shalmaneser IV	782–773 B.C.	
Ashur-dan III	773–754 B.C.	
Ashur-nirari V	754–745 B.C.	
Tiglath-pileser III (Tukulti-apil-Ešarra III, or Tiglath-pilneser, or Pul(u))	745–727 B.C.	2 Kgs 15:19,29; 16:7-10
Shalmaneser V (Ululai)	727–722 B.C.	2 Kgs 17:1-6
Sargon II	721–705 B.C.	
Sennacherib (Sin-abho-eriba)	704–681 B.C.	2 Kgs 18–19
Esarhaddon	681–669 B.C.	
Ashurbanipal	669–633 B.C.	
Ashur-etil-ilani	633–622 B.C.	
Sin-shur-ishkun	621–612 B.C.	
Ashur-uballit	612–608 B.C.	

BABYLONIAN RULERS

RULER	DATES OF RULE	SCRIPTURE REFERENCE
Merodach-Baladan II (Marduk-apal-iddin)	721–689 B.C.	2 Kgs 20:12; Isa 39:1
Nabopolassar	625–605 B.C.	
Nebuchadnezzar II (Nebuchadrezzar II)	605–562 B.C.	2 Kgs 24–25; Dan 1–4
Evil-Merodach (Amel-Marduk)	562–560 B.C.	2 Kgs 25:27-30; Jer 52:31-34
Nergal-Sharezer (Nergal-shar-usur, or Neriglissar)	560–556 B.C.	Jer 39:3,13
Labashi-Marduk	556 B.C.	
Nabonidus (Nabu-na'id)	556–539 B.C.	
Belshazzar (Bel-shar-usur)	Co-regent with Nabonidus 556–539 B.C.	Dan 5; 7:1

PERSIAN RULERS

PERSIAN RULER	DATES OF RULE	SCRIPTURE REFERENCE
CYRUS	539–530 B.C.	2 Chr 36:22-23; Ezra 1; Isa 44:28; 45:1; Dan 1:21; 10:1
CAMBYSES	530–522 B.C.	
DARIUS I HYSTASPES	522–486 B.C.	Ezra 4–6; Neh 12:22; Hag 1:1; Zech 1:1,7
XERXES I (AHASUERUS)	486–465 B.C.	Ezra 4:16 Esth
ARTAXERXES I LONGIMANUS	464–423 B.C.	Ezra 4:7-23; 7; 8:1; Neh 2:1-8 (Probably ruler during the time of the prophet Malachi.)
DARIUS II NOTHUS	423–404 B.C.	
ARTAXERXES II MNEMON	404–359 B.C.	
ARTAXERXES III OCHUS	359–338 B.C.	
ARSES	338–335 B.C.	
DARIUS III CODOMANUS	335–331 B.C.	

THE CHARACTERISTICS OF GOD PRESENTED IN THE PSALMS	
CHARACTERISTICS	**SELECTED PASSAGES**
Anger	5:6; 6:1; 27:9; 30:5; 73:20; 76:7,10; 89:38; 103:8; 106:29,32,40; 108:11; 145:8
Avenger	9:12; 24:5; 26:1; 53:5; 58:6; 59:4; 68:21-25; 72:4; 86:17; 112:8; 139:19
Creator	8:3; 24:2; 78:69; 86:9; 93:1; 95:4; 96:5; 119:73,90-91; 121:2; 124:8; 136:5-9
Deliverer (Savior)	7:1,10; 9:14; 24:5; 27:9; 37:39; 39:8; 71:2; 80:2; 119:41,94,123,146,173; 132:16
Faithful	40:10; 54:5; 91:4; 92:2; 94:14; 98:3; 100:5; 115:1; 119:75; 143:1
Forgiving	25:11; 32:5; 65:3; 78:38; 79:9; 85:2; 86:5; 99:8; 103:3,12; 130:3-4
Glory	8:1; 24:7; 26:8; 29:1; 63:2; 66:2; 79:9; 89:17; 97:6; 106:20; 113:4; 115:1; 138:5
Good	13:6; 25:7; 27:13; 31:19; 34:8; 73:1; 86:5,17; 100:5; 106:1: 119:65, 68; 125:4; 145:7,9
Gracious	67:1; 86:15; 103:8; 111:4; 112:4; 116:5; 119:58; 145:8
Healer	6:2; 30:2; 103:3; 107:20; 147:3
Holy	20:6; 22:3; 29:2; 30:4; 68:5,35; 71:22; 77:13; 78:41; 89:18,35; 99:3,5,9
Jealous	78:58; 79:5
Judge	7:8,11; 9:4,7-8; 50:4,6; 75:2,7; 98:9; 103:6; 110:6
Justice	7:6; 9:8,16; 33:5; 36:6; 67:4; 96:10; 99:4; 101:1; 103:6; 140:12
King	5:2; 9:7; 11:4; 44:4; 47:2-9; 66:7; 68:24; 74:12; 89:14; 96:10; 97:1; 145:1,11-13
Living	18:46; 42:2; 84:2

THE CHARACTERISTICS OF GOD PRESENTED IN THE PSALMS	
CHARACTERISTICS	**SELECTED PASSAGES**
Love	6:4; 21:7; 25:6; 47:4; 48:9; 52:8; 60:5; 62:12; 66:20; 98:3; 103:4,8,11,17; 106:1,45; 117:2; 119:41,64
Majesty	8:1; 68:34; 76:4; 93:1; 96:6; 104:1; 111:3; 145:5
Mercy	4:1; 5:7; 9:13; 26:11; 30:10; 31:9; 41:4,10; 57:1; 78:38; 116:1
Only God	18:31; 35:10; 73:25; 95:3; 96:4-5; 97:7; 113:5; 135:5
Perfect	18:30; 92:15
Present	16:11; 23:4; 35:22; 38:21; 48:3; 73:23; 89:15; 105:4; 110:5; 114:7; 139:7-12
Protector	3:3; 5:11; 7:10; 33:20; 66:9; 97:10; 115:9; 127:1; 145:20
Provider	67:6; 68:9; 78:23-29; 81:16; 85:12; 107:9,35-38; 132:15; 136:25; 144:12-15; 145:15
Redeemer	19:14; 25:22; 107:2; 119:134,154; 130:8
Refuge, Rock	7:1; 14:6; 19:14; 27:1; 28:1; 42:9; 62:1,8; 73:28; 89:26; 91:2,9; 92:15; 118:8
Repent	90:13; 106:45
Righteousness	4:1; 11:7; 36:6; 50:6; 72:1; 89:14; 96:13; 111:3; 119:40; 129:4
Shepherd	23:1; 28:9; 74:1; 77:20; 78:52; 79:13; 80:1; 95:7; 100:3
Spirit	51:11; 104:30; 139:7; 143:10
Universal	24:1; 50:1,12; 59:13; 65:2,5; 66:4; 68:32; 69:34; 86:9; 96:1,7; 99:2-3; 100:1; 138:4; 150:6
Wisdom	104:24; 136:5; 147:5
Wonder Worker	40:5; 46:8; 65:5; 66:3,5; 68:7-8; 72:18; 73:28; 74:13; 78:4; 81:10; 86:8,10; 98:1; 107:8,15; 135:8-9; 136:4,10-16; 145:4

-48-

CITIES OF JOSHUA'S CONQUEST

City	Scripture	Occupants	Comments
Gilgal	4:19—5:15	Unoccupied?	No battle; became worship center
Jericho	6:1-27	Canaanites	Rahab spared; oldest walled city; Achan sinned
Ai	7:1—8:29	Amorites	Israel defeated at first for Achan's sin; Ai means "ruin"
Shechem	8:30-35; ch. 24	Hivites (Gen. 38); patriarchs; relatives of Israel	Not conquered; became worship center
Gibeon, Chephirah, Beeroth, Kiriath-jearim	9:1—10:27	Hivites	Entered covenant with Israel to be servants at worship place
Jerusalem	10:1-27	Jebusite	Part of coalition Joshua defeated but city not conquered
Hebron	10:1-27,36-37	Amorite, but in patriarchal times Hittite; also home of Anakim (11:21)	Coalition partner whose city was destroyed; patriarchal city (Gen. 13:18); given to Caleb (14:9-13); city of refuge (20:7)
Jarmuth	10:1-27	Amorite	Coalition partner
Lachish	10:1-27,31-32	Amorite	Coalition partner whose city was destroyed
Eglon	10:1-27,34-35	Amorite	Coalition partner whose city was destroyed
Makkedah	10:16-17,28	?	Scene of battle with coalition
Libnah	10:29-30	?	Levitical city (21:13)
Gezer	10:33	Canaanite	Old, large city whose king Joshua defeated; city not occupied (Judg. 1:29); Levitical city (21:21)
Debir	10:38-39	Amorite; home of Anakim (11:21)	Captured by Joshua and Othniel (15:17); levitical city (21:15); name of King of Eglon (10:3)
Hazor	11:1-15	Canaanite	Largest city in Canaan; ancient history; head of northern coalition; destroyed by Joshua
Madon	11:1	?	Northern coalition partner Joshua defeated; Greek Septuagint calls it Meron; compare Waters of Merom

Name	Reference		Notes
Shimron	11:1	?	Has various spellings in mss; appears in ancient Egyptian sources
Achshaph	11:1	?	Means "place of sorcery"; mentioned in ancient Egyptian sources
Geder	12:13	?	Mystery city unknown elsewhere; sometimes seen as scribe's notation for city of longer name
Hormah	12:14	?	Southern border city (Num. 14:45); defeated by Simeon and Judah (Judg. 1:1,17)
Arad	12:14	Canaanites	Defeated by Moses (Num. 21:1-3) and named Hormah; occupied by Kenites (Judg. 1:16-17)
Adullam	12:15	?	Patriarchal ties (Gen. 38)
Bethel	12:16	?	Strong patriarchal ties (Gen. 12; 28; 35); means "house of God," associated with Ai (7:2); Joseph defeated it (Judg. 1:22-25)
Tappuah	12:17	?	Border city between Ephraim and Manasseh (16:8; 17:7-8)
Hepher	12:17	?	Name of a clan in Manasseh (17:1-2; compare Num. 26:28-37)
Aphek	12:18	?	In ancient Egyptian sources; compare 1 Sam. 4; 29)
Lasharon	12:18	?	Unusual Hebrew construction; means, "of Sharon;" may modify Aphek
Taanach	12:21	Canaanite	In ancient Egyptian sources; levitical city (21:25); Manasseh could not occupy it (Judg. 1:27)
Megiddo	12:21	Canaanite	Major ancient city guarding military pass; in Egyptian sources; Manasseh could not occupy (Judg. 1:27)
Kedesh	12:22	?	City of refuge (20:7); levitical city (21:32); home of Barak (Judg. 4:6)
Jokneam	12:22	?	Also spelled Jokmeam; levitical city (21:34); in Egyptian sources
Dor	12:23; compare 11:2	Associated with sea peoples in Egyptian records	Manasseh could not occupy (17:11-13; Judg. 1:27)
Goiim in Gilgal	12:23	Name means "nations"	Compare Gen. 14:1; uncertain scribal reading in text; appears to be in Galilee
Tirzah	12:24	Canaanite	Ancient city; became capital of Israel (1 Kings 14:17); see Song of Sol 6:4

COVENANTS AND LAW CODES
(2nd Millennium B.C.)

LAW CODE			COVENANT *
Title	Identifies superior partner.		Title
Prologue	Shows how the superior partner has cared for the subordinate one in the past, thereby inspiring gratitude and obedience within the subordinate partner.		Prologue
Laws	Lists the laws given by the superior partner which are to be obeyed by the subordinate partner		Stipulations/Laws
Blessings and Curses		Provides for the preservation of the text in the temple of the subordinate partner.	Depositions Reading
		Witnessed and guaranteed by the gods of both partners.	Witnesses
	Pronounces curses on those who disobey and blessings on those who obey.		Blessings and Curses
		Ratified by an oath and a ceremony, and sanctions are pronounced against any person who breaks the covenantal relationship.	Oath Ceremony Sanctions

* Covenants also follow the pattern of an ancient Near Eastern treaty. See the discussion in the introduction to the Book of Deuteronomy.

THE FAMILY OF DAVID

Boaz — — — Ruth

Obed

Jesse

Eliab	Abinadab	Shimea	Nethanel	Raddai	Ozem	Zeruiah	David	Abigail
(First Son)	(Second Son)	(Third Son)	(Fourth Son)	(Fifth Son)	(Sixth Son)		(Seventh Son)	

1 Sam 16:1-10; 1 Chr 2:13-17

-51-

Michal	Ahinoam	Abigail	Maacah	Haggith	Abital	Eglah	Bathsheba	Other	Concubines
(Wife)	(Wife)	(Wife)	(Wife?)	(Wife?)	(Wife?)	(Wife)	(Wife)	Wives	
1 Sam 18:27	1 Sam 25:43	1 Sam 25:42					2 Sam 11:1-12:25		

Amnon	Kileab (or Daniel)	Absalom	Adonijah	Shephatiah	Ithream		Other Sons 1 Chr 3:9

2 Sam 3:2-5; 1 Chr 3:1-4

Shammua	Shobab	Nathan	Solomon		Tamar	and Nine Sons

2 Sam 5:14; 2 Chr 3:5; 14:3-4

2 Sam 5:13-15; 1 Chr 3:6-9; 14:3-7

Jesus Christ
(see Matt 1:6-16)

▲ Male

⬭ Female

- - - marries

| HUMAN CHARACTERISTICS PRESENTED IN THE PSALMS ||
CHARACTERISTICS	SELECTED PASSAGES
Afflicted, Poor, Needy	12:5; 14:6; 22:26; 25:16; 34:2,6; 49:2; 68:5,10; 72:2; 74:19; 76:9; 82:3; 113:7; 136:23; 145:14
Anger	37:8; 124:3; 138:7; 139:21-22
Blessed	1:1; 2:12; 3:8; 5:12; 24:5; 34:8; 41:1; 65:4; 84:4,12; 106:3; 119:1; 129:8; 132:15; 134:3
Confident	3:5; 4:8; 27:1; 30:6; 41:11; 71:5
Covenant/Partners	25:10; 50:5,16; 74:20; 78:10,37; 89:3,28,34,39; 103:18; 105:8; 106:45; 111:5,9; 132:12
Death/Sheol	6:5; 16:10; 23:4; 31:17; 44:22; 49:9-20; 55:4,15,23; 68:20; 78:33,50; 82:7; 103:15; 104:29; 115:17
Enemies	3:1,7; 4:2; 6:10; 8:2; 9:3; 18:37,48; 27:2; 41:2,7; 66:3; 68:1,21; 78:53,61,66; 81:14; 108:12; 129:1; 132:18
Faithful, Godly	4:3; 18:25; 26:1; 31:23; 37:28; 73:1; 84:11; 85:10-11; 86:2; 97:10; 101:2; 108:1; 125:4; 139:23-24
Fool, Impious	14:1; 53:1; 74:18,22; 92:6; 94:8; 107:17
Humans, Mortal	22:6; 33:13; 49:7; 55:13; 56:4; 62:9; 82:5; 89:47; 115:16; 133:1; 139:16; 146:3
Joy	4:7; 16:9; 20:5; 21:1; 27:6; 28:7; 34:2; 47:1; 48:11; 53:6; 63:11; 68:3; 81:1; 90:14; 98:4; 100:1; 107:22; 145:7

HUMAN CHARACTERISTICS PRESENTED IN THE PSALMS

CHARACTERISTICS	SELECTED PASSAGES
King of Israel/ Anointed	2:2,6-8; 20:6; 28:8; 45:1,6; 61:6; 63:11; 78:70; 84:9; 92:10; 119:14,74; 122:5; 144:10
Kings of Earth	33:16; 48:4; 58:1; 68:12; 76:12; 94:20; 102:15; 106:41; 110:5; 119:23,46,161; 138:4; 146:3; 149:8
Loving God	5:11; 18:1; 69:36; 70:4; 91:14; 97:10; 116:1; 119:132; 145:20
Nations/Peoples	9:5,15,19; 22:27; 44:11; 46:6; 59:5; 67:2; 68:30; 72:17; 78:55; 82:8; 99:1-2; 105:1,13,38; 110:6
Righteous	5:12; 11:5; 14:5; 15:1; 17:1,15; 18:20; 23:3; 33:1; 34:15; 37:6,12,16,21,25,30; 55:22; 58:10; 68:3; 72:2; 92:12; 97:11; 106:31; 125:3; 142:7; 146:8
Sacrifice	4:5
Sin	5:10; 14:3; 18:22; 19:13; 25:7; 36:1-2; 51:1,5,13; 52:2; 58:3; 66:18; 68:21; 89:32; 99:8; 103:10,12; 106:6,13-39,43; 107:11,17
Suffering	22:24; 31:7; 38:3; 41:3; 55:3; 119:50,107,153
Trust	4:5; 9:10; 13:15; 20:7; 21:7; 22:4,9; 28:7; 37:3; 40:3; 52:8; 62:8; 84:12; 112:7; 115:9; 116:10; 125:1
Wicked	5:4; 6:8; 7:9,14; 11:2; 23:4; 26:5; 27:2; 32:10; 52:1,7; 53:1,4; 55:3; 58:3; 59:2; 68:2; 73:3; 82:4; 84:10,22; 94:3,13,16,23; 104:35; 107:34,42; 119:53,95,119,150,155; 147:6
Wisdom	90:12; 107:43; 111:10; 119:98

THE JEWISH CALENDAR

Year		Month	English Months (nearly)	Festivals	Seasons and Productions
Sacred	Civil				
1	7	Nison/Abib 30 days	April	1 New Moon 14 The Passover 15-21 Unleavened Bread	Spring rains (Deut 11:14) Floods (Josh 3:15) Barley ripe
2	8	Iyyar/Ziv 29 days	May	1 New Moon 14 Second Passover (for those unable to keep first)	**Harvest** Barley Harvest (Ruth 1:22) Wheat Harvest Summer begins No rain from April to Sept. (1 Sam 12:17)
3	9	Sivan 30 days	June	1 New Moon 6 Pentecost	
4	10	Tammuz 29 days	July	1 New Moon 17 Fast for the taking of Jerusalem	**Hot Season** Heat increases
5	11	Ab 30 days	August	1 New Moon 9 Fast for the destruction of Temple	The streams dry up Heat intense Vintage (Lev 26:5)
6	12	Elul 29 days	September	1 New Moon	Heat intense (2 Kgs 4:19) Grape harvest (Num 13:23)

7	1	Tishri/Ethanim 30 days	October	1 New Year, Day of Blowing of Trumpet Day of Judgment and Memorial (Num 29:1) 10 Day of Atonement (Lev 16) 15 Booths 21 (Lev 23:24) 22 Solemn Assembly	**Seed time** Former or early rains begin (Joel 2:23) Plowing and sowing begin
8	2	Marchesran/Bul 29 days	November	1 New Moon	Rain continues Wheat and barley sown
9	3	Chislev 30 days	December	1 New Moon 25 Dedication (John 10:22,29)	**Winter** Winter begins Snow on mountains
10	4	Tebeth 29 days	January	1 New Moon 10 Fast for the siege of Jerusalem	Coldest month Hail and snow (Josh 10:11)
11	5	Shebat 30 days	February	1 New Moon	Weather gradually warmer
12	6	Adar 29 days	March	1 New Moon 13 Fast of Esther 14-15 Purim	Thunder and hail frequent Almond tree blossoms
13	Leap year	Veadar/Adar Sheni	March/April	1 New Moon 13 Fast of Esther 14-15 Purim	Intercalary Month

Note 1 The Jewish year is strictly lunar, being 12 lunations with an average 29-1/2 days making 354 days in the year.
The Jewish sacred year begins with the new moon of spring, which comes between our March 22 and April 25 in cycles of 19 years.
We can understand it best if we imagine our New Year's Day, which now comes on January 1 without regard to the moon, varying each year with the moon, the time of the Passover, or the time of the full moon which, as a new moon, had introduced the New Year two weeks before.

Note 2 Hence the Jewish calendar contains a 13th month, Veadar or Adar Sheni, introduced 7 times in every 19 years, to render the average length of the year nearly correct and to keep the seasons in the proper months.

Note 3 The Jewish day begins at sunset of the previous day.

JEWISH FEASTS AND FESTIVALS

NAME	MONTH: DATE	REFERENCE	SIGNIFICANCE
Passover	Nisan (Mar./Apr.): 14-21	Exod 12:2-20; Lev 23:5	Commemorates God's deliverance of Israel out of Egypt.
Feast of Unleavened Bread	Nisan (Mar./Apr.): 15-21	Lev 23:6-8	Commemorates God's deliverance of Israel out of Egypt. Includes a Day of Firstfruits for the barley harvest.
Feast of Weeks, or Harvest (Pentecost)	Sivan (May/June): 6 (seven weeks after Passover)	Exod 23:16; 34:22; Lev 23:15-21	Commemorates the giving of the law at Mount Sinai. Includes a Day of Firstfruits for the wheat harvest.
Feast of Trumpets (Rosh Hashanah)	Tishri (Sept./Oct.): 1	Lev 23:23-25 Num 29:1-6	Day of the blowing of the trumpets to signal the beginning of the civil new year.
Day of Atonement (Yom Kippur)	Tishri (Sept./Oct.): 10	Lev 23:26-32; Exod 30:10	On this day the high priest makes atonement for the nation's sin. Also a day of fasting.
Feast of Booths, or Tabernacles (Sukkot)	Tishri (Sept./Oct.): 15-21	Lev 23:33-43; Num 29:12-39; Deut 16:13	Commemorates the forty years of wilderness wandering.
Feast of Dedication, or Festival of Lights (Hanukkah)	Kislev (Nov./Dec.): 25-30, and Tebeth (Dec./Jan.): 1-2	John 10:22	Commemorates the purification of the temple by Judas Maccabaeus in 164 B.C.
Feast of Purim, or Esther	Adar (Feb./Mar.): 14	Esth 9	Commemorates the deliverance of the Jewish people in the days of Esther.

JUDGES OF THE OLD TESTAMENT

NAME	REFERENCE	IDENTIFICATION
Othniel	Judg 1:12-13; 3:7-11	Conquered a Canaanite city
Ehud	Judg 3:12-30	Killed Eglon, king of Moab, and defeated Moabites
Shamgar	Judg 3:31	Killed 600 Philistines with an oxgoad
Deborah	Judg 4–5	Convinced Barak to lead an army to victory against Sisera's troops
Gideon	Judg 6–8	Led 300 men to victory against 135,000 Midianites
Tola	Judg 10:1-2	Judged for 23 years
Jair	Judg 10:3-5	Judged for 22 years
Jephthah	Judg 11:1–12:7	Defeated the Ammonites after making a promise to the Lord
Ibzan	Judg 12:8-10	Judged for 7 years
Elon	Judg 12:11-12	Judged for 10 years
Abdon	Judg 12:13-15	Judged for 8 years
Samson	Judg 13–16	Killed 1,000 Philistines with a donkey's jawbone; was deceived by Delilah; destroyed a Philistine temple; judged 20 years
Samuel	1 and 2 Sam	Was the last of the judges and the first of the prophets

LIFE OF ABRAHAM

EVENT	OLD TESTAMENT PASSAGE	NEW TESTAMENT REFERENCE
The birth of Abram	Gen 11:26	
God's call of Abram	Gen 12:1-3	Heb 11:8
The entry into Canaan	Gen 12:4-9	
Abram in Egypt	Gen 12:10-20	
Lot separates from Abram	Gen 13:1-18	
Abram rescues Lot	Gen 14:1-17	
Abram pays tithes to Melchizedek	Gen 14:18-24	Heb 7:1-10
God's covenant with Abraham	Gen 15:1-21	Rom 4:1-25 Gal 3:6-25 Heb 6:13-20
The birth of Ishmael	Gen 16:1-16	
Abraham promised a son by Sarah	Gen 17:1-27	Rom 4:18-25 Heb 11:11-12
Abraham intercedes for Sodom	Gen 18:16-33	
Lot saved and Sodom destroyed	Gen 19:1-38	
The birth of Isaac	Gen 21:1-7	
Hagar and Ishmael sent away	Gen 21:8-21	Gal 4:21-31
Abraham challenged to offer Isaac as sacrifice	Gen 22:1-19	Heb 11:17-19 Jas 2:20-24
The death of Sarah	Gen 23:1-20	
The death of Abraham	Gen 25:1-11	

MESSIANIC PROPHECIES OF THE OLD TESTAMENT

PROPHECY	OT REFERENCES	NT FULFILLMENT
Seed of the woman	Gen 3:15	Gal 4:4; Heb 2:14
Nations blessed through Abraham	Gen 12:3;18:18; 22:18; 26:4; 28:14	Matt 1:1; Acts 3:25; Gal 3:8
Seed of Abraham	Gen 12:7; 13:15; 15:18; 17:7-10; 23:7	Acts 7:5; Rom 4:13,16; 9:8; Gal 3:16,29
Seed of Isaac	Gen 17:19; 21:12; 26:3-4	Rom 9:7; Heb 11:18
Of the tribe of Judah	Gen 49:10	Heb 7:14; Rev 5:5
Lamb slain for us	Exod 12:1-11; Isa 53:7	John 1:29-36, 19:36; 1 Cor 5:7-8; Rev 5:6-14, 7:14; 21:22-27; 22:1-4
No bone broken	Exod 12:46; Num 9:12; Ps 34:20	John 19:36
Firstborn son sanctified	Exod 13:2; Num 3:13; 8:17	Luke 2:23
Serpent in wilderness	Num 21:8-9	John 3:14-15
A star out of Jacob	Num 24:17-19	Matt 2:2
Prophet like Moses	Deut 18:15,18-19	Matt 21:11; Luke 7:16,39; 24:19; John 1:21,25John 6:14; 7:40; Acts 3:22-23
Cursed on the tree	Deut 21:23	Gal 3:13
The throne of David established forever	2 Sam 7:12-13,16,25-26 1 Kings 11:36; 1 Chr 17:11-14, 23-27; 2 Chr 21:7 Ps 89:3-4, 36-37; 132:10-12; Isa 9:7	Matt 19:28; 25:31; Luke 1:32; Acts 2:30; 13:23; Rom 1:3; 2 Tim 2:8; Heb 1:8; 8:1; 12:2; Rev 22:1
A promised Redeemer	Job 19:25-27	Gal 4:4-5
Raise Gentile opposition	Ps 2:1-2	Acts 4:25-26
Declared to be the Son of God	Ps 2:7; Pro 30:4	Matt 3:17; Mark 1:11; Luke 1:35; Acts 13:33; Heb 1:5; 5:5; 2 Pet 1:17
Break Gentiles with rod	Ps 2:9	Rev 2:26-27; 12:5; 19:15-16
His resurrection	Ps 16:8-10; 49:15; 86:13	Acts 2:27; 13:35
Felt forsaken by God	Ps 22:1	Matt 27:46; Mark 15:34
Mocked and insulted	Ps 22:7-8, 17	Matt 27:39-43; Mark 15:29-32; Luke 23:35-39
Thirsty	Ps 22:15; 69:21	John 19:28
Hands and feet pierced	Ps 22:16	Matt 27:31,35-36
Soldiers cast lots for coat	Ps 22:18	Matt 27:35; Mark 15:20,24; Luke 23:34; John 19:23-24
Accused by false witnesses	Ps 27:12; 35:11	Matt 26:60-61; Mark 14:55-61
He commits His spirit	Ps 31:5	Luke 23:46
No broken bone	Ps 34:20	John 19:36
Hated without reason	Ps 35:19; 69:4	John 15:24-25
Friends stand afar off	Ps 38:11; 88:18	Matt 27:55; Mark 15:40; Luke 23:49
"I come to do Thy will"	Ps 40:6-8	Heb 10:5-9
Betrayed by a friend	Ps 41:9; 55:12-14	Matt 26:14-16,23,47-50; Mark 14:17-21; Luke 22:19-23; John 13:18-19
King known for righteousness	Ps 45:1-7	Heb 1:8-9
Blessed by nations	Ps 72:17	Luke 1:48
His ascension	Ps 68:18	Eph 4:8
Stung by reproaches	Ps 69:9	Rom 15:3
Zeal for God's house	Ps 69:9	John 2:17
Given gall and vinegar	Ps 69:21	Matt 27:34,48; Mark 15:23,36; Luke 23:36; John 19:29
Care for needy	Ps 72:13	Luke 10:33
He speaks in parables	Ps 78:2	Matt 13:34-35
Make Him my firstborn	Ps 89:27	Rom 8:29; Col 1:15,18; Heb 1:6
"Thou remainest"	Ps 102:24-27	Heb 1:10-12
Prays for His enemies	Ps 109:4	Matt 5:44; Luke 23:34
Another to succeed Judas	Ps 109:7-8	Acts 1:16-20
David's Lord at God's right hand	Ps 110:1	Matt 22:41-45; 26:64; Mark 12:35-37; 16:19; Acts 7:56; Eph 1:20; Col 3:1; Heb 1:3,13; 8:1; 10:12; 12:2
A priest like Melchizedek	Ps 110:4	Heb 5:6,10; 6:20; 7:1-22; 8:1; 10:11-13
The chief cornerstone	Ps 118:22-23	Matt 21:42; Mark 12:10-11; Luke 20:17; Acts 4:11; Eph 2:20; 1 Pet 2:4-7
The King comes in the name of the Lord	Ps 118:26	Matt 21:9; 23:39; Mark 11:9; Luke 13:35; 19:38; John 12:13
Repentance for the nations	Isa 2:2-4	Luke 24:47
Hearts are hardened	Isa 6:9-10	Matt 13:14-15; John 12:39-40; Acts 28:25-27
Born of a virgin	Isa 7:14	Matt 1:22-23; Luke 1:27-35
A rock of offense	Isa 8:14,15	Rom 9:33; 1 Pet 2:8
Light out of darkness	Isa 9:1-2	Matt 4:14-16; Luke 2:32
Immanuel, God with us	Isa 7:14; 8:8,10	Matt 1:21,23; John 14:8-10; 14:19; Col 2:9
Son to be given	Isa 9:6	John 3:16
Government on His shoulders	Isa 9:6	Matt 28:18; 1 Cor 15:24-25

MESSIANIC PROPHECIES OF THE OLD TESTAMENT

PROPHECY	OT REFERENCES	NT FULFILLMENT
Spirit of the Lord on Him	Isa 11:2; 42:1	Matt 3:16; Mark 1:10; Luke 3:22; John 1:32; 3:34
Full of wisdom and power	Isa 11:1-10	Rom 15:12; 1 Cor 1:30; Eph 1:17; Col 2:3
Reigning in mercy	Isa 16:4-5	Luke 1:31-33
Key of David	Isa 22:21-25	Rev 3:7
Death swallowed up in victory	Isa 25:6-12	1 Cor 15:54
A stone in Zion	Isa 28:16	Rom 9:33; 1 Pet 2:6
The deaf hear, the blind see	Isa 29:18-19	Matt 11:5; Mark 7:37; John 9:39
Healing for the needy	Isa 35:4-10	Matt 9:30; 11:5; 12:22; 20:34; 21:14; Mark 7:31-35; John 9:1-7
Make ready the way of the Lord	Isa 40:3-5	Matt 3:3; Mark 1:3; Luke 3:4-5; John 1:23
The Shepherd tends His sheep	Isa 40:10-11	John 10:11; Heb 13:20; 1 Pet 2:25
The meek Servant	Isa 42:1-4	Matt 12:17-21; Phil 2:7
A light to the Gentiles	Isa 49:6	Luke 2:32; Acts 13:47; 26:23
Scourged and spat upon	Isa 50:6	Matt 26:67; 27:26,30; Mark 14:65; 15:15,19; Luke 22:63-65; John 19:1
Rejected and insulted	Isa 53:3	Matt 27:1-2,12-14,39; Luke 18:31-33; John 1:10-11
Suffered vicariously	Isa 53:4-5	Matt 8:17; Mark 15:3-4,27-28; Luke 23:1-25,32-34
Pierced for our transgressions	Isa 53:5	Rom 4:25; 5:6,8; 1 Cor 15:3; 2 Cor 5:21
Lamb slaughtered for us	Isa 53:7	John 1:29,36; Acts 8:28-35; 1 Pet 1:19; Rev 5:6; 13:8
Silent when accused	Isa 53:7	Matt 26:63; 27:12,14; Mark 14:61; 15:5; Luke 23:9; John 19:9
Buried with the rich	Isa 53:9	Matt 27:57-60
Bear Iniquities and give forgivness	Isa 53:11	Acts 10:43; 13:38-39; 1 Cor 15:3; Eph 1:7; 1 Pet 2:21-25; 1 John 1:7,9
Crucified with transgressors	Isa 53:12	Mark 15:27-28; Luke 22:37
Calling of Gentiles	Isa 55:4-5	Rom 9:25-26; Rev 1:5
Deliver out of Zion	Isa 59:16-20	Rom 11:26-27
Nations walk in the light	Isa 60:1-3	Luke 2:32
Anointed to preach liberty	Isa 61:1-3	Luke 4:17-19; Acts 10:38
Called by a new name	Isa 62:1-2	Rev 2:17; 3:12
The King cometh	Isa 62:11	Matt 21:5; Rev 22:12
A vesture dipped in blood	Isa 63:1-3	Rev 19:13
Afflicted with the afflicted	Isa 63:8-9	Matt 25:34-40
New heavens and a new earth	Isa 65:17-25	2 Pet 3:13; Rev 21:1
The Lord our righteousness	Jer 23:5-6; 33:16	Rom 3:22; 1 Cor 1:30; 2 Cor 5:21; Phil 3:9
Born a King	Jer 30:9	Luke 1:69; John 18:37; Acts 13:23; Rev 1:5
Massacre of infants	Jer 31:15	Matt 2:17-18
A New Covenant	Jer 31:31-34	Matt 26:27-29; Mark 14:22-24; Luke 22:15-20; 1 Cor 11:25; Heb 8:8-12 10:15-17; 12:24; 13:20
A tree planted by God	Ezek 17:22-24	Matt 13:31-32
The humble exalted	Ezek 21:26-27	Luke 1:52
The good Shepherd	Ezek 34:23-24	John 10:11
His kingdom triumphant	Dan 2:44-45	Luke 1:33; 1 Cor 15:24; 2 Pet 1:11; Rev 11:15
Son of Man in power	Dan 7:13-14	Matt 24:30; 25:31; 26:64; Mark 13:26; 14:61-62; Luke 21:27; Acts 1:9-11; Rev 1:7
Kingdom for the saints	Dan 7:27	Luke 1:33; 1 Cor 15:24; Rev 11:15; 20:4; 22:5
Israel restored	Hos 3:5	Rom 11:25-27
Flight into Egypt	Hos 11:1	Matt 2:15
Promise of the Spirit	Joel 2:28-32	Acts 2:17-21;
The sun darkened	Amos 8:9	Matt 24:29; Acts 2:20; Rev 6:12
Restoration of David's house	Amos 9:11-12	Acts 15:16-18
The kingdom established	Isa. 2:1-4; Mic 4:1-8	Luke 1:33
Born in Bethlehem	Mic 5:1-5	Matt 2:1-6; Luke 2:4,10-11
Earth filled with knowledge of the glory of the Lord	Hab 2:14	Rev 21:23-26
God living among His people	Zech 2:10-13	Rev 21:3,24
A new priesthood	Zech 3:8	Eph 2:20-21; 1 Pet 2:5
Enthroned High Priest	Zech 6:12-13	Heb 5:5-10; 7:11-28; 8:1,2
Triumphal entry	Zech 9:9-10	Matt 21:4-5; Mark 11:1-10; Luke 19:28-38; John 12:13-15
Sold for thirty pieces of silver	Zech 11:12-13	Matt 26:14-15
Money buys potter's field	Zech 11:12-13	Matt 27:9-10
Piercing of His body	Zech 12:10	John 19:34,37
Shepherd smitten—sheep scattered	Zech 13:1,6-7	Matt 26:31; John 16:32
Preceded by Forerunner	Mal 3:1	Matt 11:10; Mark 1:2; Luke 7:27
The sun of righteousness	Mal 4:2-3	Luke 1:78; Eph 5:14; 2 Pet 1:19; Rev 2:28; 19:11-12; 22:16
The coming of Elijah	Mal 4:5-6	Matt 11:14; 17:10-12; Mark 9:11-13; Luke 1:17

MUSICAL INSTRUMENTS OF THE OLD TESTAMENT

TYPE	NAME	SCRIPTURE REFERENCES	LANGUAGE OF ORIGIN	NIV TRANSLATION
PERCUSSION	Bagpipe	Dan 3:5,7,10,15	Aramaic: *sumponeyah*	pipes
	Bells	(1) Exod 28:33-34; 39:25-26 (2) Zech 14:20	(1) Hebrew: *paamon* (2) Hebrew: *metsilloth*	(1) bells (2) bells of the horses
	Cymbals	(1) 2 Sam 6:5; Ps 150:5 (2) 1 Chr 13:8;15:16,19; 2 Chr 5:12-13; Ezra 3:10; Neh 12:27	(1) Hebrew: *tseltselim* (2) Hebrew: *metsiltayim*	(1) cymbals (2) cymbals
	Sistrum	2 Sam 6:5	Hebrew: *menaanim*	sistrums
	Tambourine	Gen 31:27; Exod 15:20; Judg 11:34; 1 Sam 10:5; 18:6; 2 Sam 6:5; 1 Chr 13:8; Job 21:12; Pss 81:2; 149:3; Isa 5:12; Jer 31:4	Hebrew: *toph*	tambourine
STRING	Harp	(1) 1 Sam 10:5; Neh 12:27; Isa 5:12; 14:11; Amos 5:23; 6:5 (2) Dan 3:5,7,10,15	(1) Hebrew: *nebel* (2) Aramaic: *pesanterin*	(1) lyres, harp(s) (2) harp
	Harplike Instrument	Dan 3:5,7,10,15	Aramaic: *sabbeka*	harp
	Lyre	(1) Gen 4:21; 1 Sam 10:5; 2 Sam 6:5; Neh 12:27 (2) Dan 3:5,7,10,15	(1) Hebrew: *kinnor* (2) Aramaic: *qitharos, qathros*	(1) harp (2) zither
	Zither	Pss 33:2; 92:3; 144:9	Hebrew: *nebel asor*	ten-stringed lyre
WIND	Double Pipe	1 Sam 10:5; 1 Kgs 1:40; Isa 5:12; Jer 48:36	Hebrew: *chalil*	flutes
	Horn, Cornet	Dan 3:5,7,10,15	Aramaic: *qeren*	horn
	Pipe, Reed	Dan 3:5,7,10,15	Aramaic: *mashroqitha*	flute
	Ram's Horn	(1) Josh 6:4-20; Judg 7:16-22; 2 Sam 15:10; Pss 47:5; 150:3; Amos 2:2 (2) Exod 19:13	(1) Hebrew: *shophar* (2) Aramaic: *yobel*	(1) rams' horns, trumpets (2) ram's horn
	Trumpet	(1) Num 10:2-10; 1 Chr 15:24,28; 2 Chr 15:14; 23:13; Ps 98:6; Hos 5:8 (2) Ezek 7:14	(1) Hebrew: *chatsotsrah* (2) Hebrew: *taqoa*	(1) trumpet (2) trumpet
	Vertical Flute	Gen 4:21; Job 21:12; 30:3; Ps 150:4	Hebrew: *uggab*	flute

PRIESTS IN THE OLD TESTAMENT
(Listed alphabetically)

NAME	REFERENCE	IDENTIFICATION
Aaron	Exod 28–29	Older brother of Moses; first high priest of Israel
Abiathar	1 Sam 22:20-23; 2 Sam 20:25	Son of Ahimelech who escaped the slayings at Nob
Abihu	See Nadab and Abihu	
Ahimelech	1 Sam 21–22	Led a priestly community at Nob; killed by Saul for befriending David
Amariah	2 Chr 19:11	High priest during the reign of Jehoshaphat
Amaziah	Amos 7:10-17	Evil priest of Bethel; confronted Amos the prophet
Azariah	2 Chr 26:16-20	High priest who stood against Uzziah when the ruler began to act as a prophet
Eleazar and Ithamar	Lev 10:6; Num 20:26	Godly sons of Aaron; Eleazar—Israel's second high priest
Eli	1 Sam 1–4	Descendant of Ithamar; raised Samuel at Shiloh
Eliashib	Neh 3:1; 13:4-5	High priest during the time of Nehemiah
Elishama and Jehoram	2 Chr 17:7-9	Teaching priests during the reign of Jehoshaphat
Ezra	Ezra 7–10; Neh 8	Scribe, teacher, and priest during the rebuilding of Jerusalem after the Babylonian captivity
Hilkiah	2 Kgs 22–23	High priest during the reign of Josiah
Hophni and Phinehas	1 Sam 2:12-36	Evil sons of Eli
Ithamar	See Eleazar and Ithamar	
Jahaziel	2 Chr 20:14-17	Levite who assured Jehoshaphat of deliverance from an enemy
Jehoiada	2 Kgs 11–12	High priest who saved Joash from Queen Athaliah's purge
Jehoram	See Eliashama and Jehoram	
Joshua	Hag 1:1,12; Zech 3	First high priest after the Babylonian captivity
Nadab and Abihu	Lev 10:1-2	Evil sons of Aaron
Pashhur	Jer 20:1-6	False priest who persecuted the prophet Jeremiah
Phinehas	(1) Num 25:7-13 (2) See Hophni and Phinehas	(1) Son of Eleazar; Israel's third high priest whose zeal for pure worship stopped a plague
Shelemiah	Neh 13:13	Priest during the time of Nehemiah; was in charge of administrating storehouses
Uriah	2 Kgs 16:10-16	Priest who built pagan altar for evil King Ahaz
Zadok	2 Sam 15; 1 Kgs 1	High priest during the reign of David and Solomon

CHARTS

-62-

THE PROPHETS IN HISTORY
(9th—5th century B.C.)

Prophet	Approximate Dates (B.C.)	Location/ Home	Basic Bible Passage	Central Teaching	Key Verse
Elijah	875–850	Tishbe	1 Kgs 17:1–2 Kgs 2:18	Yahweh, not Baal, is God	1 Kgs 18:21
Micaiah	856	Samaria	1 Kgs 22; 2 Chr 18	Judgment on Ahab; Proof of prophecy	1 Kgs 22:28
Elisha	855–800	Abel Meholah	1 Kgs 19:15-21; 2 Kgs 2–9; 13	God's miraculous power	2 Kgs 5:15
Jonah	786-746	Gath Hepher	2 Kgs 14:25; Jonah	God's universal concern	Jonah 4:11
Hosea	786-746	Israel	Hosea	God's unquenchable love	Hos 11:8-9
Amos	760-750	Tekoa	Amos	God's call for justice and righteousness	Amos 5:24
Isaiah	740–698	Jerusalem	2 Kgs 19–20; Isaiah	Hope through repentance & suffering	Isa 1:18; 53:4-6
Micah	735–710	Moresheth Gath Jerusalem	Jer 26:18; Micah	Call for humble mercy and justice	Mic 6:8
Oded	733	Samaria	2 Chr 28:9-11	Do not go beyond God's command	2 Chr 28:9
Nahum	686-612	Elkosh	Nahum	God's jealousy protects His people	Nah 1:2-3
Zephaniah	640-621	?	Zephaniah	Hope for the humble righteous	Zeph 2:3
Jeremiah	626–584	Anathoth/ Jerusalem	2 Chr 36:12; Jeremiah	Faithful prophet points to new covenant	Jer 31:33-34
Huldah (the prophetess)	621	Jerusalem	2 Kgs 22; 2 Chr 34	God's Book is accurate	2 Kgs 22:16
Habakkuk	608-598	?	Habakkuk	God calls for faithfulness	Hab 2:4
Ezekiel	593–571	Babylon	Ezekiel	Future hope for new community of worship	Ezek 37:12-13
Obadiah	580	Jerusalem	Obadiah	Doom on Edom to bring God's kingdom	Obad 21
Joel	539-331	Jerusalem	Joel	Call to repent and experience God's Spirit	Joel 2:28-29
Haggai	520	Jerusalem	Ezra 5:1; 6:14; Haggai	The priority of God's house	Hag 2:8-9
Zechariah	520–514	Jerusalem	Ezra 5:1; 6:14; Zechariah	Faithfulness will lead to God's universal rule	Zech 14:9
Malachi	500-450	Jerusalem	Malachi	Honor God and wait for His righteousness	Mal 4:2

QUEENS OF THE OLD TESTAMENT
(Listed alphabetically)

NAME	REFERENCE	IDENTIFICATION
Abijah	2 Kgs 18:2	Mother of King Hezekiah of Judah
Athaliah	2 Kgs 11	Evil daughter of Ahab and Jezebel; mother of King Ahaziah of Judah (only woman to rule Judah in her own right)
Azubah	1 Kgs 22:42	Mother of King Jehoshaphat of Judah
Bathsheba	2 Sam 11–12; 1 Kgs 1–2	Wife of Uriah, then wife of David and mother of Solomon
Esther	Esth 2–9	Jewish wife of King Ahasuerus of Persia
Hamutal	2 Kgs 23:31; 24:18	Mother of King Jehoahaz and King Zedekiah of Judah
Hephzibah	2 Kgs 21:1	Mother of King Manasseh of Judah
Jecoliah	2 Kgs 15:2	Mother of King Azariah of Judah
Jedidah	2 Kgs 22:1	Mother of King Josiah of Judah
Jehoaddin	2 Kgs 14:2	Mother of King Amaziah of Judah
Jezebel	1 Kgs 16:31; 18:13,19; 19:1-2; 21:1-25; 2 Kgs 9:30-37	Evil wife of King Ahab of Israel (who promoted Baal worship, persecuted God's prophets, and planned Naboth's murder)
Maacah	1 Kgs 15:10; 2 Chr 15:16	Mother of King Abijah and grandmother of King Asa of Judah
Meshullemeth	2 Kgs 21:19	Mother of King Amon of Judah
Michal	1 Sam 18:20-28; 26:44; 2 Sam 3:13-16; 6:20-23	Daughter of Saul and first wife of David
Naamah	1 Kgs 14:21,31	Mother of King Rehoboam of Judah
Nehushta	2 Kgs 24:8	Mother of King Jehoiachin of Judah
Queen of Sheba	1 Kgs 10:1-13	Foreign queen who visited Solomon
Zebidah	2 Kgs 23:36	Mother of King Jehoiakim of Judah

THE RETURN FROM EXILE

PHASE	DATE	SCRIPTURE REFERENCE	JEWISH LEADER	PERSIAN RULER	EXTENT OF THE RETURN	EVENTS OF THE RETURN
FIRST	538 B.C.	Ezra 1–6	Zerubbabel Jeshua	Cyrus	(1) Anyone who wanted to return could go. (2) The temple in Jerusalem was to be rebuilt. (3) Royal treasury provided funding of the temple rebuilding. (4) Gold and silver worship articles taken from temple by Nebuchadnezzar were returned.	(1) Burnt offerings were made. (2) The Feast of Tabernacles was celebrated. (3) The rebuilding of the temple was begun. (4) Persian ruler ordered rebuilding to be ceased. (5) Darius, King of Persia, ordered rebuilding to be resumed in 520 B.C. (6) Temple was completed and dedicated in 516 B.C.
SECOND	458 B.C.	Ezra 7–10	Ezra	Artaxerxes Longimanus	(1) Anyone who wanted to return could go. (2) Royal treasury provided funding. (3) Jewish civil magistrates and judges were allowed.	Men of Israel intermarried with foreign women.
THIRD	444 B.C.	Nehemiah 1–13	Nehemiah	Artaxerxes Longimanus	Rebuilding of Jerusalem was allowed.	(1) Rebuilding of wall of Jerusalem was opposed by Sanballat the Horonite, Tobiah the Ammonite, and Geshem the Arab. (2) Rebuilding of wall was completed in 52 days. (3) Walls were dedicated. (4) Ezra read the Book of the Law to the people. (5) Nehemiah initiated reforms.

C
H
A
R
T
S

-64-

RULERS OF OLD TESTAMENT PAGAN NATIONS
(Listed Alphabetically)

NAME	REFERENCE	NATIONALITY
Abimelech	(1) Gen 20	Philistine
	(2) Gen 26	Philistine
Achish	1 Sam 21:10-14; 27–29	Philistine
Adoni-Zedek	Josh 10:1-27	Canaanite
Agag	1 Sam 15:8-33	Amalekite
Ahasuerus	See Xerxes I	
Ammon, King of (Unnamed)	Judg 11:12-28	Ammonite
Artaxerxes	Ezra 4:7-23; 7; 8:1; Neh 2:1-8	Persian/Mede
Ashurbanipal (also known as Osnapper)	Ezra 4:10	Assyrian
Baalis	Jer 40:14	Ammonite
Balak	Num 22–24	Moabite
Belshazzar	Dan 5; 7:1	Babylonian
Ben-Hadad I	1 Kgs 20:1-34	Syrian
Ben-Hadad II	2 Kgs 6:24	Syrian
Bera	Gen 14:2-24	Canaanite
Cyrus the Great	2 Chron 36:22-23; Ezra 1; Isa 44:28; 45:1; Dan 1:21; 10:1	Persian/Mede
Darius the Great	Ezra 4–6; Neh 12:22; Hag 1:1; Zech 1:1,17	Persian/Mede
Darius the Mede	Dan 11:1	Persian/Mede
Edom, King of (Unnamed)	Num 20:14-21	Edomite
Eglon	Judg 3:12-30	Moabite
Egypt, Pharaoh of (Unnamed)	(1) Gen 12:18-20	Egyptian
	(2) Gen 41:38-55	Egyptian
	(3) Exod 1:8	Egyptian
	(4) Exod 2:15	Egyptian
	(5) Exod 3:10; 5:1	Egyptian
	(6) 1 Kgs 3:1	Egyptian
Esarhaddon	Ezra 4:2	Assyrian
Evil-Merodach	2 Kgs 25:27-30; Jer 52:31-34	Babylonian
Hanun	2 Sam 10:1-4	Ammonite
Hazael	1 Kgs 19:15; 2 Kgs 8:7-15	Syrian
Hiram	1 Kgs 5:1-18	Tyrian
Hophra	Jer 44:30	Egyptian
Jabin	(1) Josh 11:1-11	Canaanite
	(2) Judg 4:2	Canaanite
Jericho, King of (Unnamed)	Josh 2:2	Canaanite
Merodach-Baladan	2 Kgs 20:12; Isa 39:1	Babylonian
Mesha	2 Kgs 3:4-27	Moabite
Nahash	1 Sam 11:12	Ammonite
Nebuchadnezzar	2 Kgs 24–25; Dan 1–4	Babylonian
Neco	2 Kgs 23:29-30	Egyptian
Nergal-Sherezer	Jer 39:3,13	Babylonian
Osnapper	SEE Ashurbanipal	
Pul	SEE Tiglath-Pileser III	
Rezin	2 Kgs 15:37; 16:5-9	Syrian
Sargon II	Isa 20	Assyrian
Sennacherib	2 Kgs 18–19; Isa 36–37	Assyrian
Shalmaneser V	2 Kgs 17:1-6	Assyrian
Shishak	1 Kgs 14:25-26; 2 Chr 12:2-9	Egyptian
Tiglath-Pileser III	2 Kgs 15:19,29; 16:7-10	Assyrian
Tyre, Prince of (Unnamed)	Ezek 28:1-10	Tyrian
Xerxes I (also known as Ahasuerus)	Ezra 4:6; Esth	Persian/Mede

RULERS OF ISRAEL AND JUDAH

RULERS OF THE UNITED KINGDOM

Saul 1 Sam 9:1–31:13
David 1 Sam 16:1–1 Kgs 2:11
Solomon 1 Kgs 1:1–11:43

RULERS OF THE DIVIDED KINGDOM

RULERS OF ISRAEL		RULERS OF JUDAH	
Jeroboam I	I Kgs 11:26–14:20	Rehoboam	1 Kgs 11:42–14:31
		Abijah (Abijam)	1 Kgs 14:31–15:8
Nadab	1 Kgs 15:25-28	Asa	Kgs 15:8-24
Baasha	1 Kgs 15:27–16:7		
Elah	1 Kgs 16:6-14		
Zimri	1 Kgs 16:9-20		
Omri	1 Kgs 16:15-28		
Ahab	1 Kgs 16:28–22:40	Jehoshaphat	1 Kgs 22:41-50
Ahaziah	1 Kgs 22:40–2 Kgs 1:18	Jehoram	2 Kgs 8:16-24
Jehoram (Joram)	2 Kgs 1:17–9:26	Ahaziah	2 Kgs 8:24–9:29
Jehu	2 Kgs 9:1-10:36	Athaliah	2 Kgs 11:1-20
Jehoahaz	2 Kgs 13:1-9	Joash	2 Kgs 11:1–12:21
Jehoash (Joash)	2 Kgs 13:10–14:16	Amaziah	2 Kgs 14:1-20
Jeroboam II	2 Kgs 14:23-29	Azariah (Uzziah)	2 Kgs14:21; 15:1-7
Zechariah	2 Kgs 14:29–15:12		
Shallum	2 Kgs 15:10-15	Jotham	2 Kgs 15:32-38
Menahem	2 Kgs 15:14-22		
Pekahiah	2 Kgs 15:22-26		
Pekah	2 Kgs 15:25-31	Ahaz (Jehoahaz)	2 Kgs 16:1-20
Hoshea	2 Kgs 15:30–17:6	Hezekiah	2 Kgs 18:1–20:21
		Manasseh	2 Kgs 21:1-18
		Amon	2 Kgs 21:19-26
		Josiah	2 Kgs 21:26–23:30
		Jehoahaz II (Shallum)	2 Kgs 23:30-33
		Jehoiakim (Eliakim)	2 Kgs 23:34–24:5
		Jehoiachin (Jeconiah)	2 Kgs 24:6-16; 25:27-30
		Zedekiah (Mattaniah)	2 Kgs 24:17–25:7

SACRIFICIAL SYSTEM

NAME	REFERENCE	ELEMENTS	SIGNIFICANCE
Burnt Offering	Lev 1; 6:8-13	Bull, ram, male goat, male dove, or young pigeon without blemish. (Always male animals, but species of animal varied according to individual's economic status.)	Voluntary. Signifies propitiation for sin and complete surrender, devotion, and commitment to God.
Grain Offering Also called Meal, or Tribute, Offering	Lev 2; 6:14-23	Flour, bread, or grain made with olive oil and salt (always unleavened); or incense.	Voluntary. Signifies thanksgiving for firstfruits.
Fellowship Offering Also called Peace Offering: includes (1) Thank Offering, (2) Vow Offering, and (3) Freewill Offering	Lev 3; 7:11-36; 22:17-30; 27	Any animal without blemish. (Species of animal varied according to individual's economic status.) (1) Can be grain offering.	Voluntary. Symbolizes fellowship with God. (1) Signifies thankfulness for a specific blessing; (2) offers a ritual expression of a vow; and (3) symbolizes general thankfulness (to be brought to one of three required religious services).
Sin Offering	Lev 4:1–5:13; 6:24-30; 12:6-8	Male or female animal without blemish—as follows: bull for high priest or congregation; male goat for king; female goat or lamb for common person; dove or pigeon for slightly poor; tenth of an ephah of flour for the very poor.	Mandatory. Made by one who had sinned unintentionally or was unclean in order to attain purification.
Guilt Offering	Lev 5:14–6:7; 7:1-6; 14:12-18	Ram or lamb without blemish	Mandatory. Made by a person who had either deprived another of his rights or had desecrated something holy. Made by lepers for purification.

THE TEN PLAGUES OF EGYPT

PLAGUE	SCRIPTURE
1. WATER TO BLOOD—The waters of the Nile turned to blood.	Exod 7:14-25
2. FROGS—Frogs infested the land of Egypt.	Exod 8:1-15
3. GNATS (Mosquitoes)—Small stinging insects infested the land of Egypt.	Exod 8:16-19
4. FLIES—Swarms of flies, possibly a biting variety, infested the land of Egypt.	Exod 8:20-32
5. PLAGUE ON THE CATTLE—A serious disease, possibly anthrax, infested the cattle belonging to Egyptians.	Exod 9:1-7
6. BOILS—A skin disease infected the Egyptians.	Exod 9:8-12
7. HAIL—A storm that destroyed the grain fields of Egypt but spared the land of Goshen inhabited by the Israelites.	Exod 9:13-35
8. LOCUSTS—An infestation of locusts stripped the land of Egypt of plant life.	Exod 10:1-20
9. DARKNESS—A deep darkness covered the land of Egypt for three days.	Exod 10:21-29
10. DEATH OF THE FIRSTBORN—The firstborn of every Egyptian family died.	Exod 11:1–12:30

THE TEN COMMANDMENTS

COMMANDMENT	PASSAGE	RELATED OLD TESTAMENT PASSAGES	RELATED NEW TESTAMENT PASSAGES	JESUS' TEACHINGS
You shall have no other gods before me	Exod 20:3; Deut 5:7	Exod 34:14; Deut 6:4,13-14; 2 Kgs 17:35; Ps 81:9; Jer 25:6; 35:15	Acts 5:29	Matt 4:10; 6:33; 22:37-40
You shall not make for yourself an idol	Exod 20:4-6; Deut 5:8-10	Exod 20:23; 32:8; 34:17; Lev 19:4; Lev 26:1; Deut 4:15-20; 7:25; 32:21; Ps 115:4-7; Isa 44:12-20	Acts 17:29; 1 Cor 8:4-6, 10-14; 1 John 5:21	Matt 6:24; Luke 16:13
You shall not misuse the name of the Lord	Exod 20:7; Deut 5:11	Exod 22:28; Lev 18:21; 19:12; 22:2; 24:16; Ezek 39:7	Rom 2:23-24; Jas 5:12	Matt 5:33-37; 6:9; 23:16-22
Remember the Sabbath day by keeping it holy	Exod 20:8-11; Deut 5:12-15	Gen 2:3; Exod 16:23-30; 31:13-16; 35:2-3; Lev 19:30; Isa 56:2; Jer 17:21-27	Acts 20:7; Heb 10:25	Matt 12:1-13; Mark 2:23-27; 3:1-6; Luke 6:1-11; John 5:1-18
Honor your father and your mother	Exod 20:12; Deut 5:16	Exod 21:17; Lev 19:3; Deut 21:18-21; 27:16; Prov 6:20	Eph 6:1-3; Col 3:20	Matt 15:4-6; 19:19; Mark 7:9-13; Luke 2:51; 18:20; John 19:26-27
You shall not murder	Exod 20:13; Deut 5:17	Gen 9:6; Lev 24:17; Num 35:33	Rom 13:9-10; I Pet 4:15	Matt 5:21-24; 19:18; 26:52; Mark 10:19; Luke 18:20
You shall not commit adultery	Exod 20:14; Deut 5:18	Lev 18:20; 20:10; Deut 22:22; Num 5:12-31; Prov 6:29,32	Rom 13:9-10; 1 Cor 6:9; Heb 13:4; Jas 2:11	Matt 5:27-30; 19:18; Mark 10:19; Luke 18:20; John 8:1-11
You shall not steal	Exod 20:15; Deut 5:19	Lev 19:11,13; Exek 18:7	Rom 13:9-10; Eph 4:28; Jas 5:4	Matt 19:18; Mark 10:19;12:40 Luke 18:20
You shall not give false testimony	Exod 20:16; Deut 5:20	Exod 23:1, 7; Lev 19:11; Pss 15:2; 101:5; Prov 10:18; Jer 9:3-5; Zech 8:16	Eph 4:25,31; Col 3:9; Titus 3:2	Matt 5:37; 19:18; Mark 10:19; Luke 18:20
You shall not covet	Exod 20:17; Deut 5:21	Deut 7:25; Job 31:24-28; Ps 62:10	Rom 7:7; 13:9; Eph 5:3-5; Heb 13:5; Jas 4:1-2	Luke 12:15-34

CHARTS

NEW TESTAMENT
CHARTS

CONTROVERSY STORIES IN MARK

Controversy	Reference in Mark
Over Jesus' right to forgive sins	2:1-12
Over Jesus' fellowship with tax collectors and "sinners"	2:13-17
Over the disciples' freedom from fasting	2:18-22
Over the disciples' picking grain on the Sabbath	2:23-27
Over Jesus' right to do good on the Sabbath	3:1-6
Over the nature of Jesus' family	3:20-21,31-35
Over the source of Jesus' power to exorcise	3:22-30
Over the disciples' eating with unwashed hands	7:1-5,14-23
Over the Pharisees' and teachers' of the law setting aside the commands of God in order to observe their own tradition	7:6-13
Over the legality of divorce and God's intention for marriage	10:1-12
Over Jesus' authority to cleanse the temple and John's authority to baptize	11:27-33
Over paying taxes to Caesar and giving God His due	12:13-17
Over marriage at the resurrection, the power of God, and the witness of Scripture	12:18-27
Over the most important commandment	12:28-34
Over the nature of the Messiah—son of David or David's Lord	12:35-37

DISCIPLES OF JESUS

Matthew 10:2-4	Mark 3:16-19	Luke 6:13-16	Acts 1:13-14
Simon Peter	Simon Peter	Simon Peter	Peter
Andrew	James son of Zebedee	Andrew	John
James son of Zebedee	John	James	James
John	Andrew	John	Andrew
Philip	Philip	Andrew	Philip
Bartholomew	Bartholomew	Philip	Thomas
Thomas	Matthew	Bartholomew	Bartholomew
Matthew the tax collector	Thomas	Matthew	Matthew
James son of Alphaeus	James son of Alphaeus	Thomas	James son of Alphaeus
Thaddaeus	Thaddaeus the Zealot	James son of Alphaeus	Simon the Zealot
Simon the Zealot	Simon the Zealot (compare John 14:22)	Simon who was called	Judas son of James
Judas Iscariot	Judas Iscariot	Judas son of James	(Judas Iscariot) Matthias (v. 26)

DISCOURSES OF JESUS

Where Delivered	Nature or Style	To Whom Addressed	The Lesson to Be Learned	References
1. Jerusalem	Conversation	Nicodemus	We must be "born of water and the Spirit" to enter the kingdom	John 3:1-21
2. At Jacob's Well	Conversation	Samaritan Woman	"God is spirit" to be worshiped in spirit and truth	John 4:1-30
3. At Jacob's Well	Conversation	The Disciples	Our food is to do His will	John 4:31-38
4. Nazareth	Sermon	Worshipers	No prophet is welcomed in his own hometown	Luke 4:16-30
5. Mountain of Galilee	Sermon	The Disciples and the People	The Beatitudes; to let our light shine before men; Christians the light of the world; how to pray; benevolence and humility; heavenly and earthly treasures contrasted; golden rule	Matt 5–7; Luke 6:17-49
6. Bethesda—A Pool	Conversation	The Jews	To hear Him and believe on Him is to have everlasting life	John 5:1-47
7. Galilee	Conversation	The Pharisees	Works of necessity not wrong on the Sabbath	Matt 12:1-14 Luke 6:1-11
8. Galilee	Eulogy and Denunciation	The People	Greatness of the least in heaven; judged according to the light we have	Matt 11:2-29; Luke 7:18-35
9. Galilee	Conversation	The Pharisees	The unforgivable sin is to sin against the Holy Spirit	Mark 3:19-30; Matt 12:22-45
10. Galilee	Conversation	The Disciples	The providence of God; nearness of Christ to those who serve Him	Mark 6:6-13; Matt 10:1-42
11. Galilee	Conversation	A Messenger	Relationship of those doing His will	Matt 12:46-50; Mark 3:31-35
12. Capernaum	Sermon	The Multitude	Christ as the Bread of life	John 6:22-71
13. Genessaret	Criticism and Reproof	The Scribes and Pharisees	Not outward conditions, but that which proceeds from the heart defiles	Matt 15:1-20; Mark 7:1-23
14. Capernaum	Example	The Disciples	Humility the mark of greatness; be not a stumbling block	Matt 18:1-14; Mark 9:33-50
15. Temple–Jerusalem	Instruction	The Jews	Judge not according to outward appearance	John 7:11-40
16. Temple–Jerusalem	Instruction	The Jews	To follow Christ is to walk in the light	John 8:12-59
17. Jerusalem	Instruction	The Jews	Christ the door; He knows His sheep; He gives His life for them	John 10:1-21
18. Capernaum	Charge	The Seventy	Need for Christian service; not to despise Christ's ministers	Luke 10:1-24
19. Unknown	Instruction	The Disciples	The efficacy of earnest prayer	Luke 11:1-13
20. Unknown	Conversation	The People	Hear and keep God's will; the state of the backslider	Luke 11:14-36
21. House of Pharisee	Reproof	The Pharisees	The meaning of inward purity	Luke 11:37-54
22. Unknown	Exhortation	The Multitude	Beware of hypocrisy; covetousness; blasphemy; be watchful	Luke 12:1-21
23. Unknown	Object Lesson	The Disciples	Watchfulness; the kingdom of God is of first importance	Luke 12:22-34
24. Jerusalem	Exhortation	The People	Death for life; way of eternal life	John 12:20-50
25. Jerusalem	Denunciation	The Pharisees	Avoid hypocrisy and pretense	Matt 23:1-39
26. Mount of Olives	Prophecy	The Disciples	Signs of the coming of the Son of man; beware of false prophets	Matt 24:1-51; Mark 13:1-37
27. Jerusalem	Exhortation	The Disciples	The lesson of humility and service	John 13:1-20
28. Jerusalem	Exhortation	The Disciples	The proof of discipleship; that He will come again	John 14–16

-74-

DOCTRINAL EMPHASES IN THE LETTERS OF PAUL

Paul's Letters	Purpose	Major Doctrine(s)	Key Passage	Other Key Doctrines	Notes on the Letter
Romans	To express the nature of the Gospel, its relation to the OT and Jewish law, and its transforming power	Salvation	Rom 3:21-26	God Humanity The Church	Martin Luther (1515), through preparing lectures on Romans, felt himself "to be reborn."
1 Corinthians	To respond to questions about marriage, idol food, public worship; to discourage factions, to instruct on resurrection	The Church The Resurrection	1 Cor 12:12-31 1 Cor 15:1-11	God Humanity	The hymn on love in Chapter 13 is among the most familiar and loved chapters in Paul's writings.
2 Corinthians	To prepare readers for Paul's third visit and to defend Paul and the gospel he taught against false teachers	The Church Jesus Christ Salvation	2 Cor 5:11–6:2	God	Called by C.K. Barrett "the fullest and most passionate account of what Paul meant by apostleship."
Galatians	To stress freedom in Christ against Jewish legalism while avoiding moral license	Salvation	Gal 2:15-21	Christian Ethics The Church Election	Called the "Magna Charta" of Christian liberty.
Ephesians	To explain God's eternal purpose and grace and the goals God has for the church	Salvation The Church	Eph 2:1-22 Eph 3:14-21	God Jesus Christ	Called by Samuel Taylor Coleridge "one of the divinest of compositions."
Philippians	To commend Epaphroditus; to affirm generosity; to encourage unity, humility, and faithfulness even to death	Christian Unity Joy in Salvation	Phil 1:3-11	Christian Ethics The Church Prayer	Bengel (1850) described as "Summa epistlae, gaudes, gaudete," which means "The sum of the epistles is 'I rejoice; rejoice ye.'"
Colossians	To oppose false teachings related to a matter and spirit dualism and stress the complete adequacy of Christ	Jesus Christ	Col 1:15-23	The Church Prayer God	Arius of Alexandria (318) used Col 1:15, from a hymn on the supremacy of Christ, to undermine Christ's deity. Arianism pronounced heretical at Councils of Nicea (325) and Constantinople (381).

Paul's Letters	Purpose	Major Doctrine(s)	Key Passage	Other Key Doctrines	Notes on the Letter
1 Thessalonians	To encourage new converts during persecution; to instruct them in Christian living and to assure them concerning the second coming	Last Things	1 Thess 4:13-18	Evangelism Prayer God	Every chapter of 1 Thessalonians ends with a reference to the second coming.
2 Thessalonians	To encourage new converts in persecution and to correct misunderstandings about the Lord's return	Last Things	2 Thess 1:3-12	Prayer The Church Evil & Suffering	With only three chapters, the letter is one of Paul's shortest yet because of 2:3-10 one of the most extensively studied.
1 Timothy	To encourage Timothy as minister, to refute false doctrine, and to instruct about church organization and leadership	Church Leaders	1 Tim 3:1-15	God Christian Ethics Salvation	Known as a "pastoral epistle" since the early part of the eighteenth century, Thomas Aquinas (d.1274) described 1 Timothy as a "pastoral textbook."
2 Timothy	To encourage Christians in the face of persecution and false doctrine	Education	2 Tim 2:14-19	Evil & Suffering Jesus Christ Prayer	Used by Augustine (d.430) in book four on Christian Doctrine to support the importance of Christian teachers.
Titus	To instruct church leaders, to advise about groups in the church, and to teach Christian ethics	Salvation	Titus 2:11-14	God Christian Ethics The Church Sin	This letter is a pastor's guide against heresy.
Philemon	To effect reconciliation between a runaway slave and his Christian master	Christian Ethics	Phlm 8–16	Prayer The Church Discipleship	Called by Emil Brunner (d.1965) a classic testimony to what is meant by Christian justice.

-75-

A HARMONY OF THE GOSPELS

PART: I. INTRODUCTORY STATEMENTS

	Matt.	Mark	Luke	John
1. Luke's Historical Introduction			1:1-4	
2. John's Theological Introduction				1:1-18
3. Matthew's and Luke's Genealogical Introductions	1:1-17		3:23-58	

PART II. THE BIRTH AND YOUTH OF JOHN THE BAPTIST AND JESUS

	Matt.	Mark	Luke	John
4. The Annunciation to Zacharias Place: Jerusalem			1:5-25	
5. The Annunciation to the Virgin Mary Place: Nazareth			1:26-38	
6. Songs of Elizabeth and Mary Place: Judea			1:39-56	
7. Birth and Youth of John the Baptist Place: Judea			1:57-80	
8. The Annunciation to Joseph Place: Nazareth	1:18-25			
9. The Birth of Jesus Place: Bethlehem			2:1-7	
10. The Angel and Shepherds Place: Near Bethlehem			2:8-20	
11. Circumcision and Naming of Jesus Place: Bethlehem			2:21	
12. The Presentation in the Temple Place: Jerusalem			2:22-38	
13. The Visit of the Wise Men Place: Jerusalem, Bethlehem	2:1-12			
14. Flight to Egypt and Return to Nazareth Place: Nazareth, Egypt	2:13-23		2:39	
15. His Youth in Nazareth and Visit to Jerusalem Place: Nazareth, Jerusalem			2:40-52	

PART III. JOHN THE BAPTIST'S MINISTRY

	Matt.	Mark	Luke	John
16. The Coming of the Word Place: Wilderness		1:1	3:1-2	

	Matt.	Mark	Luke	John
17. The Response of John in Wilderness Place: Wilderness	3:1-6	1:2-6	3:3-6	
18. The Boldness of His Preaching Place: Wilderness	3:7-10		3:7-14	
19. John's Idea of the Messiah	3:11, 12	1:7, 8	3:15-18	

PART IV. EARLY MINISTRY OF JESUS

	Matt.	Mark	Luke	John
20. The Baptism in the Jordan Place: Jordan	3:13-17	1:9-11	3:21-23	
21. The Temptation of Jesus by Satan Place: Judean Wilderness	4:1-11	1:12, 13	4:1-13	
22. Testimony of John and Disciples Place: Bethany				1:19-51
23. The First Miracle Place: Cana				2:1-11
24. The First Stay in Capernaum Place: Capernaum				2:12
25. First Passover an Cleansing Temple Place: Jerusalem				2:13-3:21
26. Closing Ministry and Arrest of John Place: Aenon			3:19, 20	3:22-36; 4:1-3
27. Jesus at Jacob's Well and Sychar Place: Samaria				4:4-42
28. Jesus Returns to Galilee Place: Galilee	4:12	1:14	4:14	4:43-45

PART V. THE MINISTRY IN GALILEE

	Matt.	Mark	Luke	John
29. The Message of Jesus—Repentance Place: Galilee	4:17	1:15	4:15	
30. Healing the Centurion's Son Place: Capernaum				4:46-54
31. Jesus Rejected by the People Place: Nazareth	4:13-16		4:16-31	
32. Calling the Fishermen Place: Capernaum	4:18-22	1:16-20	5:1-11	
33. A Busy Sabbath in Capernaum Place: Capernaum	8:14-17	1:21-34	4:32-41	
34. The First Tour of Galilee Place: Galilee	4:23-25	1:35-39	4:42-44	
35. The Healing of a Leper Place: Galilee	8:2-4	1:40-45	5:12-16	
36. Healing the Paralytic in Peter's Home Place: Capernaum	9:1-8	2:1-12	5:17-26	
37. The Call of Matthew (Levi) Place: Sea of Galilee	9:9-13	2:13-17	5:27-32	
38. Three Parables About Fasting Place: The Seaside	9:14-17	2:18-22	5:33-39	

	Matt.	Mark	Luke	John
39. First Sabbath Controversy in Jerusalem Place: Jerusalem				5:1-47
40. Further Controversies in Galilee Place: Galilee	12:1-14	2:23-3:6	6:1-11	
41. Choosing the Twelve Place: Near Capernaum	5:1—8:1	3:14-19	6:12-49	
42. Healing the Centurion's Servant Place: Capernaum	8:5-13		7:1-10	
43. Raising the Son of a Widow Place: Nain			7:11-17	
44. Doubt of John and Praise of Jesus Place: Nain	11:2-19		7:18-35	
45. The Cities of Opportunity Place: Capernaum	11:20-30			
46. The Sinful Woman in House of Simon Place: Capernaum			7:36-50	
47. Jesus and Disciples Go to Galilee			8:1-3	
48. Jesus Accused of Blasphemy Place: Galilee	12:15-45	3:19-30		
49. The Mother of Jesus Calls Him	12:46-50	3:31-35	8:19-21	
50. The First Extended Group of Parables Place: Sea of Galilee	13:1-53	4:1-34	8:4-18	
51. Jesus Stills the Storm and Heals Demoniac Place: Sea of Galilee; Gadara	8:23-34	4:35–5:20	8:22-39	
52. Healing Jairus' Daughter and Woman with Issue of Blood Place: Capernaum	9:18-26	5:21-43	8:40-56	
53. Two Blind Men and Demoniac Healed Place: Capernaum	9:27-34			
54. Last Rejection at Nazareth Place: Nazareth	13:54-58	6:1-6		
55. The Disciples Given Power to Heal Place: Capernaum	10:1-42	6:6-13	9:1-6	
56. Herod Fears John and Jesus	14:1-12	6:14-29	9:7-9	

PART VI. THE WITHDRAWAL FROM GALILEE

	Matt.	Mark	Luke	John
57. First Withdrawal to Bethsaida-Julias	14:13-21	6:30-44	9:10-17	6:1-13
58. The Return to Gennesaret Place: Lake of Gennesaret	14:22-36	6:45-56		6:14-21
59. Rejection of Christ in the Synagogue Place: Capernaum				6:22-71
60. Criticism of the Pharisees Concerning Unwashed Hands Place: Capernaum	15:1-20	7:1-23		7:1
61. Healing Daughter of Syrophoenecian Place: Phoenicia	15:21-28	7:24-30		

	Matt.	Mark	Luke	John
62. Jesus Departs to Sea of Galilee	15:29-38	7:31-8:9		
63. Pharisees and Sadducees Attack Jesus, Again Asking a Sign Place: Dalmanutha or Magadan	15:39-16:4	8:10-12		
64. Jesus Again Withdraws to Bethsaida-Julias Place: Bethsaida	16:5-12	8:13-26		
65. The Great Confession of Peter Place: Caesarea-Philippi	16:13-20	8:27-30	9:18-21	
66. Jesus Predicts His Death and Resurrection Place: Galilee	16:21-28	8:31-38	9:22-27	
67. The Transfiguration of Jesus Place: Mt. Tabor	17:1-13	9:2-13	9:28-36	
68. Disciples Unable to Cast Out Evil Spirit	17:14-21	9:14-29	9:37-42	
69. Further Reference to His Death and Resurrection Place: Galilee	17:22-23	9:30-32	9:43-45	
70. Jesus Pays Tax by Miracle Place: Capernaum	17:24-27			
71. Disciples Contending Who Is Greatest Place: Capernaum	18:1-5	9:33-37	9:46-48	
72. Jesus Rebukes the Narrowness of John Place: Capernaum	18:6-14	9:38-50	9:49-50	
73. On Forgiving a Brother Place: Capernaum	18:15-35			
74. Christ Requires Full Consecration Place: Capernaum	8:19-22		9:57-62	
75. His Unbelieving Brethren Rebuked Place: Capernaum				7:2-10
76. James and John Rebuked for Anger Place: Samaria			9:51-56	

PART VII. THE MINISTRY IN JUDEA

	Matt.	Mark	Luke	John
77. At the Feast of Tabernacles Place: Jerusalem				7:11-8:11
78. Jesus the Light of the World Place: Jerusalem				8:12-59
79. Opened Eyes of Man Born Blind Place: Jerusalem				9:1-41
80. Parable of the Good Shepherd Place: Jerusalem				10:1-21
81. The Seventy Sent Out			10:1-24	
82. Parable of the Good Samaritan Place: Jerusalem			10:25-37	

	Matt.	Mark	Luke	John
83. Jesus Received by Martha and Mary Place: Bethany			10:38-42	
84. The Disciples Taught How to Pray	6:9-13		11:1-13	
85. Accused of Healing Through Beelzebub			11:14-36	
86. The Criticism of Pharisee and Lawyer			11:37-54	
87. Warning the Disciples Against the Leaven of the Pharisees			12:1-12	
88. Covetousness and Parable of Rich Man			12:13-21	
89. The Ravens and Lilies			12:22-34	
90. The Second Coming Referred to by Jesus			12:35-48	
91. Christ's Eagerness for His Baptism of Death on the Cross			12:49-59	
92. Repentance and Parable of Fig Tree			13:1-9	
93. The Infirm Woman Healed on Sabbath			13:10-21	
94. Jesus at Feast of Dedication Place: Jerusalem				10:22-39

PART VIII. THE MINISTRY IN PEREA

	Matt.	Mark	Luke	John
95. Many Believe on Jesus Place: Bethany				10:40-42
96. Asked Concerning Number of the Saved Place: Perea			13:22-35	
97. Jesus Teaches Humility and Service Place: Near Jerusalem			14:1-24	
98. To Be Christ's Disciple Requires Forsaking All Place: Jerusalem			14:25-35	
99. Christ Justifies Himself in Receiving Sinners			15:1-32	
100. Parables Concerning Stewardship			16:1-17:10	
101. The Raising of Lazarus Place: Bethany				11:1-54
102. Jesus Goes to Jerusalem for the Passover Place: Samaria, Galilee			17:11-37	
103. Parables on Prayer on Way to Jerusalem	19:1-2	10:1	18:1-4	
104. Pharisees Tempt Jesus Concerning Divorce	19:3-12	10:2-12		
105. Christ Welcoming Little Children Place: Perea	19:13-15	10:13-16	18:15-17	
106. Parable of the Rich Young Ruler	19:16-29	10:17-30	18:18-30	
107. Parable of the Laborers in Vineyard	20:1-16	10:31		

	Matt.	Mark	Luke	John
108. Jesus Again Refers to Death and Resurrection	20:17-19	10:32-34	18:31-34	
109. Selfishness of James and John	20:20-28	10:35-45		
110. Blind Bartimaeus Receives His Sight	20:29-34	10:46-52	18:35-43	
111. Zaccheus and Parable of the Minas Place: Jericho			19:1-28	

PART IX. THE LAST JERUSALEM MINISTRY

	Matt.	Mark	Luke	John
112. The Interest in Jesus and Lazarus Place: Bethany				11:55— 12:1, 9-11
113. The Challenge to the Sanhedrin Place: Jerusalem	21:1-17	11:1-11	19:29-44	12:12-19
114. Cursing the Fig Tree—Cleansing Place: Jerusalem	21:18-19	11:12-18	19:45-48	
115. The Greeks Seek Jesus While He Is in Agony of Soul Place: Jerusalem				12:20-50
116. The Withered Fig Tree, and the Power of Faith Place: Jerusalem	21:19-22	11:19-26	21:37-38	
117. Sanhedrin Questions the Authority of Jesus Place: Jerusalem	21:23-46 22:1-14	11:27— 12:12	20:1-19	
118. An Attempt to Entrap Jesus Concerning Tribute to Caesar Place: Jerusalem	22:15-22	12:13-17	20:20-26	
119. A Further Attempt to Puzzle Jesus Place: Jerusalem	22:23-33	12:18-27	20:27-40	
120. The Legal Problem of a Lawyer Place: Jerusalem	22:34-40	12:28-34		
121. Jesus Silences Enemies by Appeal to David Place: Jerusalem	22:41-46	12:35-37	20:41-44	
122. A Denunciation of Scribes and Pharisees Place: Jerusalem	23:1-39	12:38-40	20:45-47	
123. The Widow's Two Mites Place: Jerusalem		12:41-44	21:1-4	

PART X. JESUS COUNSELS HIS DISCIPLES LEADING UP TO HIS SACRIFICE

	Matt.	Mark	Luke	John
124. The Great Eschatological Discourse Place: Jerusalem	24:1—25:30		13:1-37	21:5-36
125. Jesus Predicts His Arrest Place: Jerusalem	26:1-5	14:1-2	22:1-2	

-81-

	Matt.	Mark	Luke	John
126. Jesus Anointed by Mary Place Bethany	26:6-13	14:3-9		12:2-8
127. The Act of Judas Iscariot Place: Jerusalem	26:14-16	14:10-11	22:3-6	
128. Preparation for Passover and Jealousy of the Disciples Place: Jerusalem	26:17-20	14:12-17	22:7-30	
129. Jesus Washes the Apostle's Feet Place: Jerusalem				13:1-20
130. Judas Named as the Betrayer Place: Jerusalem	26:21-25	14:18-21	22:21-23	13:21-30
131. Steadfastness of the Disciples Questioned Place: Jerusalem	26:31-35	14:27-31	22:31-38	13:34-38
132. The Memorial Supper Instituted Place: Jerusalem	26:26-29	14:22-25	22:17-20	(1 Cor. 11:23-26)
133. Jesus Opens His Heart to the Disciples Concerning His Departure Place: Upper Room and on Way to Gethsemane				14:1—16:33
134. The Intercessory Prayer Place: Near Gethsemane				17:1-26
135. The Agony in Gethsemane	26:36-40	14:32-42	22:39-46	18:1

PART XI. THE CONDEMNATION AND THE CROSS

	Matt.	Mark	Luke	John
136. The Betrayal, Arrest , and Desertion by the Disciples Place: Gethsemane	26:47-56	14:43-52	22:47-53	18:2-12
137. The Examination by Annas Place: Jerusalem				18:13-23
138. Condemned on Perjured Testimony Place: Jerusalem	26:57-68	14:53-65	22:54, 63-65	18:24,
139. Peter's Three Denials Place: Jerusalem	26:58, 69-75	14:54, 66-72	22:54-62	18:15-18, 25-27
140. An Attempt to Make the Trial Legal Place Jerusalem	27:1	15:1	22:66-71 (See Acts 1:18-19)	
141. Judas Realizes His Sin Place: Jerusalem	27:3-10			
142. Jesus Before Pilate Place: Jerusalem	27:2, 11-14	15:2-5	23:1-5	18:28-38
143. Jesus Is Sent to Herod Place: Jerusalem			23:6-12	
144. Herod Returns Jesus to Pilate Place: Jerusalem	27:15-26	15:6-15	23:13-25	18:39— 19:16
145. Jesus Is Mocked by Soldiers Place: Jerusalem	27:27-30	15:16-19		
146. Simon Bears the Cross Place: on Way to Calvary	27:31-34	15:20-23	23:26-33	19:16-17

	Matt.	Mark	Luke	John
147. Jesus Is Crucified Place: Calvary	27:35-50	15:24-37	23:33-46	19:18-30
148. The Supernatural Phenomena Place: Jerusalem	27:51-56	15:38-41	23:45-49	
149. Burial in Joseph's Tomb Place: Gethsemane	27:57-60	15:42-46	23:50-54	19:31-42
150. The Women by the Tomb	27:61-66	15:47	23:55-56	

PART XII. THE RESURRECTION AND ASCENSION

	Matt.	Mark	Luke	John
151. At the Tomb on the Sabbath Place: Gethsemane	28:1			
152. Anointing with Spices		16:1		
153. The Tomb Is Opened	28:2-4			
154. Women Find the Empty Tomb and Angels	28:5-8	16:2-8	24:1-8	20:1
155. The Women Report to the Apostles Place: Jerusalem			24:9-12	20:2-10
156. Jesus Appears to Mary Magdalene Place: Jerusalem		16:9-11		20:11-18
157. Then Other Women See Him	28:9-10			
158. The Watchmen Bribed to Claim the Body Taken by the Disciples	28:11-15			
159. Jesus Appears on Way to Emmaus		16:12-13	24:13-32	(See also 1Cor. 15:5)
160. Simon Peter Sees Jesus			24:33-35	
161. Entire Group, Except Thomas, See Him, and He Eats Before Them Place: Jerusalem		16:14	24:36-43	20:19-25
162. Entire Group, with Thomas, See Him, Finally Believing				20:26-31
163. Jesus Appears by Sea of Galilee			(See also 1 Cor. 15:6)	21:1-25
164. The Apostles Commissioned to Preach Place: Galilee	28:16-20	16:15-18	(1 Cor. 15:7)	
165. James the Brother of Jesus Sees Him				
166. Jesus and Disciples Counsel for the Last Time and Jesus Ascends Place: Olivet		16:19-20	24:44-53	(See also Acts 1:3-12)

-83-

EARLY CAESARS OF ROME

Caesar	Dates	Biblical Reference
Julius Caesar	49–44 B.C.	
Second Triumvirate	44–31 B.C.	
Augustus (Octavion)	31 B.C.–A.D. 14	Luke 2:1
Tiberius	A.D. 14–37	Luke 3:1
Caligula (Gaius)	A.D. 37–41	
Claudius	A.D. 41–54	Acts 11:28; 17:7; 18:2
Nero	A.D. 54–68	Acts 25:11; Phil 4:22
Galba, Otho, and Vitellius	A.D. 68/69	
Vespasian	A.D. 69–79	
Titus	A.D. 79–81	
Domitian	A.D. 81–96	
Nerva	A.D. 96–98	
Trajan	A.D. 98–117	
Hadrian	A.D. 117–138	

THE HASMONEAN DYNASTY

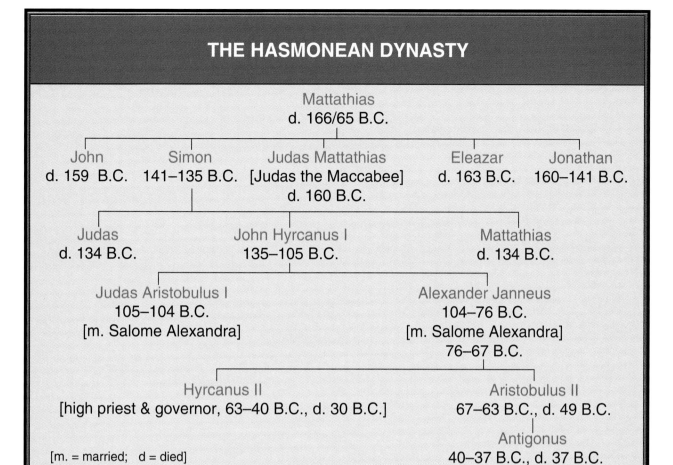

Mattathias
d. 166/65 B.C.

John	Simon	Judas Mattathias	Eleazar	Jonathan
d. 159 B.C.	141–135 B.C.	[Judas the Maccabee] d. 160 B.C.	d. 163 B.C.	160–141 B.C.

Judas	John Hyrcanus I	Mattathias
d. 134 B.C.	135–105 B.C.	d. 134 B.C.

Judas Aristobulus I	Alexander Janneus
105–104 B.C. [m. Salome Alexandra]	104–76 B.C. [m. Salome Alexandra] 76–67 B.C.

Hyrcanus II	Aristobulus II
[high priest & governor, 63–40 B.C., d. 30 B.C.]	67–63 B.C., d. 49 B.C.
	Antigonus
[m. = married; d = died]	40–37 B.C., d. 37 B.C.

-85-

THE HERODIAN RULERS

Ruler	Family Relationship	Realm of Responsibility	Dates	Biblical Reference
Herod I (the Great)	Son of Antipater	King of Judea	37–4 B.C.	Matt 2:1-22; Luke 1:5
Herod Archelaus	Oldest son of Herod the Great	Ethnarch of Judea, Samaria, and Idumea	4 B.C.–A.D. 6	Matt 2:22
Herod Philip*	Son of Herod the Great and Cleopatra of Jerusalem	Tetrarch of Iturea and Trachonitis	4 B.C.–A.D. 34	Luke 3:1
Herod Antipas	Youngest son of Herod the Great Second husband of Herodias	Tetrarch of Galilee and Perea	4 B.C.–A.D. 39	Matt 14:1-11; Mark 6:14-29; Luke 3:1,19; 13:31-33; 23:7-12
Herod Agrippa I	Grandson of Herod the Great	King of Judea	A.D. 37–44	Acts 12
Herod Agrippa II	Great-grandson of Herod the Great	Tetrarch and king of Chalcis	A.D. 44–100 (Became king in A.D. 48)	Acts 25:13–26:32

*Another Herod Philip is mentioned in the New Testament. He is the son of Herod the Great and Mariamne II and was the first husband of Herodias. (See Matt 14:3; Mark 6:17; and Luke 3:19.)

"I AM" SAYINGS IN THE GOSPEL OF JOHN

SAYING	REFERENCE IN JOHN
I am the Bread of Life.	6:35
I am the Light of the World.	8:12
I am the Gate for the Sheep.	10:7
I am the Good Shepherd.	10:11,14
I am the Resurrection and the Life.	11:25
I am the Way, the Truth, and the Life.	14:6
I am the True Vine.	15:1,5
I am a King.	18:37

JESUS' MINISTRY AS FULFILLMENT OF SCRIPTURE IN MATTHEW

Aspects of His Ministry	Fulfillment Passage in Matthew	OT Prophecy
His virgin birth and role as God with us	Matt 1:18,22-23	Isa 7:14
His birth in Bethlehem and shepherd role	Matt 2:4-6	Mic 5:2
His refugee years in Egypt and role as God's Son	Matt 2:14-15	Hos 11:1
His upbringing in Nazareth and messianic role (the Hebrew term for branch is *nezer*)	Matt 2:23	Isa 11:1
His preaching ministry in Galilee and role as Light to the Gentiles	Matt 4:12-16	Isa 9:1-2
His healing ministry and role as God's Servant	Matt 8:16-17	Isa 53:4
His reluctance to attract attention and His role as God's chosen and loved Servant	Matt 12:16-21	Isa 42:1-4
His teaching in parables and His role in proclaiming God's sovereign rule	Matt 13:34-35	Ps 78:2
His humble entry into Jerusalem and role as King	Matt 21:1-5	Zech 9:9
His betrayal, arrest, and death and role as Suffering Servant	Matt 26:50,56	The prophetic writings as a whole

TITLES FOR JESUS IN SCRIPTURE

TITLE	SIGNIFICANCE	REFERENCE
Alpha and Omega	The Beginning and Ending of all things	Rev 21:6
Bread of Life	The one essential food	John 6:35
Chief Cornerstone	A Sure Foundation of life	Eph 2:20
Chief Shepherd	Gives guidance and protection	1 Pet 5:4
Christ	The Anointed One of God foreseen by Old Testament prophets	Matt 16:16
Firstborn from the Dead	Leads us into resurrection	Col 1:18
Good Shepherd	Gives guidance and protection	John 10:11
High Priest	The Perfect Mediator	Heb 3:1
Holy One of God	Perfect and sinless	Mark 1:24
Immanuel	God with us	Matt 1:23
Jesus	His personal name meaning Yahweh Saves	Matt 1:21
King of Kings, Lord of Lords	The Sovereign Almighty	Rev 19:16
Lamb of God	Offered His life as a sacrifice for sins	John 1:29
Light of the World	One who brings hope and gives guidance	John 9:5
Lord	Sovereign Creator and Redeemer	Rom 10:9
Lord of Glory	The power of the Living God	1 Cor 2:8
Mediator	Redeemer who brings forgiven sinners into the presence of God	1 Tim 2:5
Prophet	One who speaks for God	Luke 13:33
Rabbi/Teacher	A title of respect for one who taught the Scriptures	John 3:2
Savior	One who delivers from sin	John 4:42
Son of David	One who brings in the Kingdom	Matt 9:27
Son of God	A title of Deity signifying Jesus' unique and special intimacy with the Father	John 20:31
Son of Man	A divine title of suffering and exaltation	Matt 20:28
Word	Eternal God who ultimately reveals God	John 1:1

JEWISH SECTS IN THE NEW TESTAMENT

PHARISEES

DATES OF EXISTENCE	NAME	ORIGIN	SEGMENTS OF SOCIETY
Existed under Jonathan (160–143 B.C.) Declined in power under John Hyrcanus (134–104 B.C.) Began resurgence under Salome Alexandra (76 B.C.)	Pharisees = "the Separated Ones" with three possible meanings: (1) to their separating themselves *from* people (2) to their separating themselves *to* the study of the law ("dividing" or "separating" the truth) (3) to their separating themselves *from* pagan practices	Probably spiritual descendants of the Hasidim (religious freedom fighters of the time of Judas Maccabeus)	Most numerous of the Jewish parties (or sects) Probably descendants of the Hasidim—scribes and lawyers Members of the middle class—mostly businessmen (merchants and tradesmen)

BELIEFS	SELECTED BIBLICAL REFERENCES	ACTIVITIES
Monotheistic Viewed entirety of the Old Testament (Torah, Prophets, and Writings) as authoritative Believed that the study of the law was true worship Accepted both the written and oral law More liberal in interpreting the law than were the Sadducees Quite concerned with the proper keeping of the Sabbath, tithing, and purification rituals Believed in life after death and the resurrection of the body (with divine retribution and reward) Believed in the reality of demons and angels Revered humanity and human equality Missionary-minded regarding the conversion of Gentiles Believed that individuals were responsible for how they lived	Matt 3:7-10; 5:20; 9:14; 16:1,6-12; 22:15-22,34-46; 23:2-36 Mark 3:6; 7:3–5; 8:15; 12:13-17 Luke 6:7; 7:36-39; 11:37-44; 18:9-14 John 3:1; 9:13-16; 11:46-47; 12:19 Acts 23:6-10 Phil 3:4b-6	Developers of oral tradition Taught that the way to God was through odedience to the law Changed Judaism from a religion of sacrifice to a religion of law Progressive thinkers regarding the adaptation of the law to situations Opposed Jesus because He would not accept the teachings of the oral law as binding Established and controlled synagogues Exercised great control over general population Served as religious authorities for most Jews Took several ceremonies from the temple to the home Emphasized ethical as opposed to theological action Legalistic and socially exclusive (shunned non-Pharisees as unclean) Tended to have a self-sufficient and haughty attitude

SADDUCEES

DATES OF EXISTENCE	NAME	ORIGIN	SEGMENTS OF SOCIETY
Probably began about 200 B.C. Demise occurred in A.D. 70 (with the destruction of the temple)	Sadducees = Three possible translations: (1) "the Righteous Ones"—based on the Hebrew consonants for the word *righteous* (2) "ones who sympathize with Zadok," or "Zadokites"—based on their possible link to Zadok the high priest (3) "syndics," "judges," or "fiscal controllers"—based on the Greek word *syndikoi*	Unknown origin Claimed to be descendants of Zadok—high priest under David (see 2 Sam 8:17; 15:24) and Solomon (see 1 Kgs 1:34-35; 1 Chr 12:28) Had a possible link to Aaron Were probably formed into a group about 200 B.C. as the high priest's party	Aristocracy—the rich descendants of the high-priestly line (however, not all priest were Sadducees) Possible descendants of the Hasmonean priesthood Probably not as refined as their economic position in life would suggest

BELIEFS	SELECTED BIBLICAL REFERENCES	ACTIVITIES
Accepted only the Torah (Genesis through Deuteronomy—the written law of Moses) as authoritative Practiced literal interpretation of the law Rigidly conservative toward the law Stressed strict observance of the law Observed past beliefs and tradition Opposed oral law as obligatory or binding Believed in the absolute freedom of human will—that people could do as they wished without attention from God Denied divine providence Denied the concept of life after death and the resurrection of the body Denied the concept of reward and punishment after death Denied the existence of angels and demons Materialistic	2 Sam 8:17; 15:24 1 Kgs 1:34 1 Chr 12:26-28 Ezek 40:45-46; 43:19; 44:15-16 Matt 3:7-10; 16:1,6-12; 22:23-34 Mark 12:18-27 Luke 20:27-40 John 11:47 Acts 4:1-2; 5:17-18; 23:6-10	In charge of the temple and its services Politically active Exercised great political control through the Sanhedrin, of which many were members Supported the ruling power and the status quo Leaned toward Hellenism (the spreading of Greek influence)—and were thus despised by the Jewish populace Opposed both the Pharisees and Jesus because these lived by a larger canon (The Pharisees and Jesus both considered more than only Genesis through Deuteronomy as authoritative.) Opposed Jesus specifically for fear their wealth/position would be threatened if they supported Him

ZEALOTS

DATES OF EXISTENCE	NAME	ORIGIN	SEGMENTS OF SOCIETY
Three possibilities for their beginning (1) during the reign of Herod the Great (about 37 B.C.) (2) during the revolt against Rome (A.D. 6) (3) traced back to the Hasidim or the Maccabees (about 168 B.C.) Their certain demise occurred around A.D. 70–73 with Rome's conquering of Jerusalem.	Refers to their religious zeal Josephus used the term in referring to those involved in the Jewish revolt against Rome in A.D. 6— led by Judas of Galilee	(According to Josephus) The Zealots began with Judas (the Galilean), son of Ezekias, who led a revolt in A.D. 6 because of a census done for tax purposes	The extreme wing of the Pharisees

BELIEFS	SELECTED BIBLICAL REFERENCES	ACTIVITIES
Similar to the Pharisees with this exception: believed strongly that only God had the right to rule over the Jews. Patriotism and religion became inseparable. Believed that total obedience (supported by drastic physical measures) must be apparent before God would bring in the Messianic Age Were fanatical in their Jewish faith and in their devotion to the law—to the point of martyrdom	Matt 10:4 Mark 3:18 Luke 6:15 Acts 1:13	Extremely opposed to Roman rule over Palestine Extremely opposed to peace with Rome Refused to pay taxes Demonstrated against the use of the Greek language in Palestine Engaged in terrorism against Rome and others with whom they disagreed politically (Sicarii [or Assassins] were an extremist Zealot group who carried out acts of terrorism against Rome.)

HERODIANS

DATES OF EXISTENCE	NAME	ORIGIN	SEGMENTS OF SOCIETY
Existed during the time of the Herodian dynasty (which began with Herod the Great in 37 B.C.) Uncertain demise	Based on their support of the Herodian rulers (Herod the Great or his dynasty)	Exact origin uncertain	Wealthy, politically influential Jews who supported Herod Antipas (or any descendant of Herod the Great) as ruler over Palestine (Judea and Samaria were under Roman governors at this time.)

HERODIANS (CONT.)

BELIEFS	SELECTED BIBLICAL REFERENCES	ACTIVITIES
Not a religious group—but a political one Membership probably was comprised of representatives of varied theological perspectives	Matt 22:5-22 Mark 3:6; 8:15; 12:13-17	Supported Herod and the Herodian dynasty Accepted Hellenization Accepted foreign rule

ESSENES

DATES OF EXISTENCE	NAME	ORIGIN	SEGMENTS OF SOCIETY
Probably began during Maccabean times (about 168 B.C.)—around the same time as the Pharisees and the Sadducees began to form Uncertain demise—possibly in A.D. 68–70 with the collapse of Jerusalem	Unknown origin	Possibly developed as a reaction to the corrupt Sadducean priesthood Have been identified with various groups: Hasidim, Zealots, Greek influence, or Iranian influence	Scattered throughout the villages of Judea (possibly including the community of Qumran) (According to Philo and Josephus) About 4,000 in Palestinian Syria

BELIEFS	SELECTED BIBLICAL REFERENCES	ACTIVITIES
Very strict ascetics Monastic: most took vow of celibacy (adopting male children in order to perpetuate the group), but some did marry (for the purpose of procreation) Rigidly adherent to the law (including a strict rendering of the ethical teachings) Considered other literature as authoritative (in addition to the Hebrew Scripture) Believed and lived as pacifists Rejected temple worship and temple offerings as corrupted Believed in the immortality of the soul with no bodily resurrection Apocalyptically oriented	None	Devoted to the copying and studying of the manuscripts of the law Lived in a community sense with communal property Required a long probationary period and ritual baptisms of those wishing to join Were highly virtuous and righteous Were extremely self-disciplined Were diligent manual laborers Gave great importance to daily worship Upheld rigid Sabbath laws Maintained a non-Levitical priesthood Rejected worldly pleasures as evil Rejected matrimony—but did not forbid others to marry

MILLENNIAL PERSPECTIVES ON REVELATION

POINT OF INTERPRETATION	AMILLENNIAL	HISTORICAL PREMILLENNIAL	DISPENSATIONAL PREMILLENNIAL	POSTMILLENNIAL
Description of View	Viewpoint that the present age of Christ's rule in the church is the millennium; holds to one resurrection and judgment marking the end of history as we know it and the beginning of life eternal	Viewpoint that Christ will reign on earth for a thousand years following His second coming; saints will be resurrected at the beginning of the millennium, nonbelievers at the end, followed by judgment	Viewpoint that after the battle of Armageddon, Christ will rule through the Jews for a literal thousand years accompanied by two resurrections and at least three judgments	Viewpoint that Christ will return after a long period of expansion and spiritual prosperity for the church, brought about by the preaching of the gospel; the Spirit's blessing; and the church's work toward righteousness, justice, and peace. The period is not a literal thousand years but extended time of spiritual prosperity.
Book of Revelation	Current history written in code to confound enemies and encourage Asian Christians; message applies to all Christians	Immediate application to Asian Christians; applies to all Christians throughout the ages, but the visions also apply to a great future event	"Unveiling" of theme of Christ among churches in present dispensation, also as Judge and King in dispensations to come	Written to encourage Christians of all ages, but the visions also apply to a great future event.
Seven candlesticks (1:13)	Churches		Churches, plus end-time application	Churches
Churches addressed (chaps. 2–3)	Specific historical situations, truths apply to churches throughout the ages; do not represent periods of church history		Specific historical situations and to all churches throughout the ages; shows progress of churches' spiritual state until end of church age	Specific historical situations, truths apply to churches throughout the ages; do not necessarily represent periods of church history
Twenty-four elders (4:4,10; 5:8,14)	Twelve patriarchs and twelve apostles; together symbolize all the redeemed	Company of angels who help execute God's rule (or elders represent twenty-four priestly and Levitical orders)	The rewarded church; also represents twelve patriarchs and twelve apostles	Symbolizes all the redeemed
Sealed book (5:1-9)	Scroll of history; shows God carrying out His redemptive purpose in history	Contains prophecy of end events of chapters 7–22	Title deed to the world	Portrays God carrying out His redemptive purpose in history
144,000 (7:4-8)	Redeemed on earth who will be protected against God's wrath	Church on threshold of great tribulation	Jewish converts of tribulation period who witness to Gentiles (same as 14:1)	Redeemed people of God
Great tribulation (first reference in 7:14)	Persecution faced by Asian Christians of John's time; symbolic of tribulation that occurs throughout history	Period at end time of unexplained trouble, before Christ's return; church will go through it; begins with seventh seal (18:1) which includes trumpets 1-6 (8:2–14:20)	Period at end time of unexplained trouble referred to in 7:14 and described in chapters 11–18; lasts three and a half years, the latter half of seven-year period between rapture and millennium	Symbolic of tribulation that occurs throughout history
Forty-two months (11:2); 1,260 days (11:3)	Indefinite duration of pagan desolation	A symbolic number representing period of evil with reference to last days of age	Half of seven-year tribulation period	A symbolic number representing an indefinite time and evil influence
Woman (12:1-6)	True people of God under old and new covenants (true Israel)		Indicates Israel, not church; key is comparison with Gen 37:9	True people of God under old and new covenants
Great red dragon (12:3)	All views identify as Satan			

MILLENNIAL PERSPECTIVES ON REVELATION

POINT OF INTERPRETATION	AMILLENNIAL	HISTORICAL PREMILLENNIAL	DISPENSATIONAL PREMILLENNIAL	POSTMILLENNIAL
Manchild (12:4-5)	Christ at His birth, life events, and crucifixion, whom Satan sought to kill	Christ, whose work Satan seeks to destroy	Christ but also the church (head and body); caught up on throne indicates rapture of church	Christ at His birth, life events, and crucifixion, whom Satan sought to destroy
1,260 days (12:6)	Indefinite time	Symbolic number representing period of evil with special reference to last days of age	First half of great tribula-after church is raptured	Indefinite time
Sea beast (13:1)	Emperor Domitian, personification of Roman Empire (same as in chap. 17)	Antichrist, here shown as embodiment of the four beasts in Dan 7	A new Rome, satanic federation of nations that come out of old Roman Empire	Roman Empire
Seven heads (13:1)	Roman emperors	Great power, shows kinship with dragon	Seven stages of Roman Empire; sixth was imperial Rome (John's day); last will be federation of nations	Roman Emperors
Ten horns (13:1)	Symbolize power	Kings, represent limited crowns (ten) against Christ's many	Ten powers that will combine to make the federation of nations of new Rome	Symbol of power
666 (13:18)	Imperfection, evil; personified as Domitian	Symbolic of evil, short of 777; if a personage meant, he is unknown but will be known at the proper time	Not known but will be known when time comes	Symbol of evil
144,000 on Mount Zion (14:1)	Total body of redeemed in heaven		Redeemed Jews gathered in earthly Jerusalem during millennial kingdom	Redeemed people of God
River of blood (14:20)	Symbol of infinite punishment for the wicked	Means God's radical judgment crushes evil thoroughly	Scene of wrath and carnage that will occur in Palestine	Symbol of judgment on the wicked
Babylon (woman—17:5)	Historical Rome	Capital city of future Antichrist	Apostate church of the future	Symbol of evil
Seven mountains (17:9)	Pagan Rome, which was built on seven hills	Indicate power, so here means a succession of empires, last of which is end-time Babylon	Rome, revived at end time	Pagan Rome
Seven heads (17:7) and seven kings (17:10)	Roman emperors from Augustus to Titus, excluding three brief rules	Five past godless kingdoms; sixth was Rome; seventh would arise in end time	Five distinct forms of Roman government prior to John; sixth was imperial Rome; seventh will be revived Roman Empire	Roman emperors
Ten horns (17:7) and ten kings (17:12)	Vassal kings who ruled with Rome's permission	Symbolic of earthly powers that will be subservient to Antichrist	Ten kingdoms arising in future out of revived Roman Empire	Symbolic of earthly powers
Bride, wife (19:7)	Total of all the redeemed		The church; does not include Old Testament saints or tribulation saints	Total of all the redeemed

-93-

MILLENNIAL PERSPECTIVES ON REVELATION

POINT OF INTERPRETATION	AMILLENNIAL	HISTORICAL PREMILLENNIAL	DISPENSATIONAL PREMILLENNIAL	POSTMILLENNIAL
Marriage supper (19:9)	Climax of the age; symbolizes complete union of Christ with His people	Union of Christ with His people at His Coming	Union of Christ with His church accompanied by by Old Testament saints and tribulation saints	Union of Christ with His people
One on white horse (19:11-16)	Vision of Christ's victory over pagan Rome; return of Christ occurs in connection with events of 20:7-10	Second coming of Christ		Vision of Christ's victory
Battle of Armageddon (19:19-21; see 16:16)	Not literally at end of time but symbolizes power of God's word overcoming evil; principle applies to all ages	Literal event of some kind at end time but not literal battle with military weapons; occurs at Christ's return at beginning of millennium	Literal bloody battle at Armageddon (valley of Megiddo) at end of great tribulation between kings of the East and federation of nations of new Rome; they are all defeated by blast from Christ's mouth and then millennium begins	Symbolizes power of God's Word overcoming evil forces
Great supper (19:17)	Stands in contrast to marriage supper		Concludes series of judgments and opens way for kingdom to be established	Stands in contrast to marriage supper
Binding of Satan (20:2)	Symbolic of Christ's resurrection victory over Satan	Curbing of Satan's power during the millennium		Symbolic of Christ's victory over Satan
Millennium (20:2-6)	Symbolic reference to period from Christ's first coming to His second	A historical event, though length of one thousand years may be symbolic, after Armageddon during which Christ rules with His people	A literal thousand-year period after the church age during which Christ rules with His people but especially through the Jews	A lengthy period of expansion and spiritual prosperity brought about by the preaching of the gospel
Those on thrones (20:4)	Martyrs in heaven; their presence with God is a judgment on those who killed them	Saints and martyrs who rule with Christ in the the millennium	The redeemed ruling with Christ, appearing and disappearing on earth at will to oversee life on earth	Saints and martyrs who rule with Christ
First resurrection (20:5-6)	The spiritual presence with Christ of the redeemed that occurs after physical death	Resurrection of saints at beginning of millennium when Christ returns	Includes three groups: (1) those raptured with church (4:1); (2) Jewish tribulation saints during tribulation (11:11); (3) other Jewish believers at beginning of millennium (20:5-6)	The spiritual presence of the redeemed with Christ
Second death (20:6)	Spiritual death, eternal separation from God			
New heavens and earth (21:1)	A new order; redeemed earth			
New Jerusalem (21:2-5)	God dwelling with His saints in the new age after all other end-time events			

MIRACLES OF JESUS			
MIRACLE	**BIBLE PASSAGES**		
Water Turned to Wine				John 2:1
Many Healings	Matt 4:23	Mark 1:32		
Healing of a Leper	Matt 8:1	Mark 1:40	Luke 5:12	
Healing of a Roman Centurion's Servant	Matt 8:5		Luke 7:1	
Healing of Peter's Mother-in-law	Matt 8:14	Mark 1:29	Luke 4:38	
Calming of the Storm at Sea	Matt 8:23	Mark 4:35	Luke 8:22	
Healing of the Wild Men of Gadara	Matt 8:28	Mark 5:1	Luke 8:26	
Healing of the Lame Man	Matt 9:1	Mark 2:1	Luke 5:18	
Healing of a Woman with a Hemorrhage	Matt 9:20	Mark 5:25	Luke 8:43	
Raising of Jairus's Daughter	Matt 9:23	Mark 5:22	Luke 8:41	
Healing of Two Blind Men	Matt 9:27			
Healing of a Demon-possessed Man	Matt 9:32			
Healing of Man with a Withered Hand	Matt 12:10	Mark 3:1	Luke 6:6	
Feeding of 5,000 People	Matt 14:15	Mark 6:35	Luke 9:12	John 6:1
Walking on the Sea	Matt 14:22	Mark 6:47		John 6:16
Healing of the Syrophoenician's Daughter	Matt 15:21	Mark 7:24		
Feeding of 4,000 People	Matt 15:32	Mark 8:1		
Healing of an Epileptic Boy	Matt 17:14	Mark 9:14	Luke 9:37	
Healing of Two Blind Men at Jericho	Matt 20:30			
Healing of a Man with an Unclean Spirit		Mark 1:23	Luke 4:33	
Healing of a Deaf, Speechless Man		Mark 7:31		
Healing of a Blind Man at Bethesda		Mark 8:22		
Healing of Blind Bartimaeus		Mark 10:46	Luke 18:35	
A Miraculous Catch of Fish			Luke 5:4	John 21:1
Raising of a Widow's Son			Luke 7:11	
Healing of a Stooped Woman			Luke 13:11	
Healing of a Man with the Dropsy			Luke 14:1	
Healing of Ten Lepers			Luke 17:11	
Healing of Malchus's Ear			Luke 22:50	
Healing of a Royal Official's Son				John 4:46
Healing of a Lame Man at Bethesda				John 5:1
Healing of a Blind Man				John 9:1
Raising of Lazarus				John 11:38

PARABLES OF JESUS

PARABLE	OCCASION	LESSON TAUGHT	REFERENCES
1. The speck and the log	Sermon on the Mount (Matt), Sermon on the Plain (Luke)	Do not presume to judge others	Matt 7:1-6; Luke 6:37-42
2. The two houses	Sermon on the Mount, at the close	Necessity of building life on Jesus' words	Matt 7:24-27; Luke 6:47-49
3. Children in the marketplace	Rejection of John's baptism and Jesus' ministry	Evil of a fault-finding disposition	Matt 11:16-19; Luke 7:32-34
4. The two debtors	A Pharisee's self-righteous reflections	Love to Christ proportioned to grace received	Luke 7:41-43
5. The unclean spirit	The scribes demand a miracle in the heavens	Hardening power of unbelief	Matt 12:43-45; Luke 11:24-26
6. The rich fool	Dispute of two brothers	Folly of reliance upon wealth	Luke 12:16-21
7. The barren fig tree	Tidings of the execution of certain Galileans	Still time for repentance	Luke 13:6-9
8. The sower	Sermon on the seashore	Effects of preaching religious truth	Matt 13:3-8; Mark 4:3-8; Luke 8:5-8
9. The tares	The same	The severance of good and evil	Matt 13:24-30
10. The seed	The same	Power of truth	Mark 4:26-29
11. The grain of mustard seed	The same	Small beginnings and growth of Christ's kingdom	Matt 13:31-32; Mark 4:31-32; Luke 13:19
12. The leaven	The same	Dissemination of the knowledge of Christ	Matt 13:33; Luke 13:21
13. The lamp	Sermon on the Mount (Matt), Teaching a large crowd (Mark, Luke)	Effect of good example	Matt 5:15; Mark 4:21; Luke 8:16 11:33
14. The dragnet	Sermon on the seashore	Mixed character of the church	Matt 13:47-48
15. The hidden treasure	The same	Value of God's Kingdom	Matt 13:44
16. The pearl of great value	The same	The same	Matt 13:45-46
17. The householder	The same	Varied methods of teaching truth	Matt 13:52
18. The marriage	To the critics who censured the disciples	Joy in Christ's companionship	Matt 9:15; Mark 2:19-20; Luke 5:34-35
19. The patched garment	The same	Newness of God's work in Christ, which cannot be impeded by the old	Matt 9:16; Mark 2:21; Luke 5:36
20. The wine bottles	The same	The same	Matt 9:17; Mark 2:22; Luke 5:37-38
21. The harvest	Spiritual wants of the Jewish people	Need of witness and prayer	Matt 9:37; Luke 10:2
22. The opponent	Slowness of the people to believe	Need of prompt reconciliation	Matt 5:25-26; Luke 12:58-59
23. Two insolvent debtors	Peter's question	Duty of forgiveness	Matt 18:23-35
24. The good Samaritan	The lawyer's question	The golden rule for all	Luke 10:30-37

PARABLE	OCCASION	LESSON TAUGHT	REFERENCES
25. The persistent friend	Disciples ask lesson in prayer	Effect of importunity in prayer	Luke 11:5-8
26. The good shepherd	Pharisees reject testimony of miracle	Christ the only way to God	John 10:1-16
27. The narrow, or locked, door	The question, Are there few who can be saved?	Difficulty of entry into God's Kingdom	Luke 13:24
28. The two ways	The Sermon on the Mount	Difficulty of discipleship	Matt 7:13-14
29. The guests	Eagerness to take high places	Chief places not to be usurped	Luke 14:7-11
30. The marriage supper	Self-righteous remark of a guest	Rejection of unbelievers	Matt 22:2-9; Luke 14:16-24
31. The wedding clothes	Continuation of the same discourse	Necessity of purity	Matt 22:10-14
32. The tower	Multitudes surrounding Christ	Need of counting the cost of discipleship	Luke 14:28-30
33. The king going to war	The same	The same	Luke 14:31-32
34. The lost sheep	The disciples' question; who is the greatest? (Matt), Pharisees objected to His receiving tax collectors and "sinners"	Christ's love for sinners based on God's love for them	Matt 18:12-13; Luke 15:4-7
35. The lost coin	The same	The same	Luke 15:8-9
36. The prodigal son	The same	The same	Luke 15:11-32
37. The unjust steward	To the disciples	Prudence in using property	Luke 16:1-9
38. The rich man and Lazarus	Derision of the Pharisees	Salvation not connected with wealth and the adequacy of Scripture	Luke 16:19-31
39. The importunate widow	Teaching the disciples	Perseverance in prayer	Luke 18:2-5
40. The Pharisee and tax-gatherer	Teaching the self-righteous	Humility in prayer	Luke 18:10-14
41. The slave's duty	Teaching the disciples	Humble obedience	Luke 17:7-10
42. Laborers in the vineyard	The same	God's graciously adequate gift to the unworthy	Matt 20:1-16
43. The talents	In Jerusalem (Matt) at the house of Zaccheus (Luke)	Doom of unfaithful followers	Matt 25:14-30; Luke 19:11-27
44. The two sons	The chief priests demand His authority	Obedience better than words	Matt 21:28-30
45. The wicked vine-growers	The same	Rejection of the Jewish people	Matt 21:33-43; Mark 12:1-9; Luke 20:9-15
46. The fig tree	In prophesying the destruction of Jerusalem	Duty of watching for Christ's appearance	Matt 24:32; Mark 13:28; Luke 21:29-30
47. The watching householder	The same	The same	Matt 24:43; Luke 12:39
48. The watchful slave	The same	The same	Mark 13:34-36
49. Character of two slaves	The same	Danger of unfaithfulness	Matt 24:45-51; Luke 12:42-46
50. The ten virgins	The same	Necessity of watchfulness	Matt 25:1-12
51. The watching slaves	The same	The same	Luke 12:36-38
52. The vine and branches	At the last supper	The need to abide in Christ	John 15:1-6

Spiritual Gift	Rom 12:6-8	1 Cor 12:8-10	1 Cor 12:28	1 Cor 12:29-30	Eph 4:11
PAUL'S LISTS OF SPIRITUAL GIFTS					
Apostle			1	1	1
Prophet	1	5	2	2	2
Teacher	3		3	3	5
Pastor					4
Miracles		4	4	4	
Discernment of Spirits		6			
Word of Wisdom Knowledge		1			
Evangelists					3
Encouragers		4			
Faith		2			
Healings		3	5	5	
Tongues		7	8	6	
Interpretation		8		7	
Ministry/Serving	2				
Administration			7		
Leaders	6				
Helpers			6		
Mercy	7				
Giving	5				

THE SEVEN SIGNS IN JOHN

SIGN	REFERENCE	CENTRAL TRUTH
1. Changing water to wine	2:1-11	Points to Jesus as the Source of all the blessings of God's future (see Isa 25:6-8; Jer 31:11-12; Amos 9:13-14)
2. Healing the official's son	4:43-54	Points to Jesus as the Giver of life
3. Healing the invalid at Bethesda	5:1-15	Points to Jesus as the Father's Coworker
4. Feeding the five thousand	6:1-15,25-69	Points to Jesus as the life-giving Bread from heaven
5. Walking on water	6:16-21	Points to Jesus as the divine I AM
6. Healing the man born blind	9:1-41	Points to Jesus as the Giver of spiritual sight
7. Raising Lazarus	11:1-44	Points to Jesus as the Resurrection and the Life

PAUL'S MISSION TRAVELS AND LETTERS

Book of Acts	Activity	Approximate Date	Writing
9:1-19	Paul's Conversion	34–35	
9:26-29	Visit to Jerusalem	37–38	
11:27-30	Second Visit to Jerusalem	48	
13-14	First Mission (Cyprus and Galatia)	48–50	Galatians
15	Jerusalem Council	50	
16:1–18:22	Second Mission (Galatia, Macedonia, Greece)	51–53	1, 2 Thessalonians
18:23–21:14	Third Mission (Ephesus Macedonia, Greece)	54–57	1, 2 Corinthians Romans
21:15–26:32	Arrest in Jerusalem, Trials and Imprisonment in Caesarea	58–60	
27–28	Voyage to Rome, Roman Imprisonment	60–63	Philemon Colossians Ephesians Philippians
	Release, Further Work, Final Imprisonment, and Death		1 Timothy Titus 2 Timothy

TEN MAJOR SERMONS IN ACTS

	Reference in Acts	Audience	Central Truths
	1. Acts 2:14-41	An international group of God-fearing Jews in Jerusalem for Pentecost	The gift of the Holy Spirit proves now is the age of salvation. Jesus' resurrection validates His role as Messiah.
Peter's mission sermons	2. Acts 3:11-26	A Jewish crowd in the Jerusalem temple	The healing power of Jesus' name proves that He is alive and at work. Those who rejected the Messiah in ignorance can still repent.
	3. Acts 10:27-48	The Gentile Cornelius and his household	God accepts persons of all races who respond in faith to the gospel message.
Stephen's sermon	4. Acts 7:1-60	The Sanhedrin	God revealed Himself outside the Holy Land. God's people capped a history of rejecting the leaders He had sent them by killing the Messiah.
Paul's mission sermons	5. Acts 13	Jews in the synagogue in Pisidian Antioch	Paul's mission sermons illustrate the changing focuses of early Christian mission work: first Jewish evangelism, second Gentile evangelism, third development of Christian leaders.
	6. Acts 17	Pagan Greeks at the Areopagus in Athens	
	7. Acts 20	Christian leaders of the Ephesian church	
Paul's defense sermons	8. Acts 22:1-21	Temple crowd in Jerusalem	Paul's defense sermons stressed that Paul was innocent of any breach of Roman law. Paul was on trial for his conviction that Jesus had been raised from the dead and had commissioned him as a missionary to the Gentiles.
	9. Acts 24:10-21	The Roman Governor Felix	
	10. Acts 26	The Jewish King Agrippa II	

THEMES IN LUKE

THEME	EXAMPLES FROM LUKE	REFERENCE
Theology	Word of God Jesus as Savior The present kingdom of God The Holy Spirit	5:1; 6:47; 8:11,13-15,21; 11:28 1:69; 2:11; 19:9 11:20; 19:9 1:35,41,67; 2:25-27; 3:22; 4:1,14; 11:13; 24:49

Concern for women	Elisabeth
	 Mary
	 Anna
	 The widow of Nain
	 The "sinner" who anoints Jesus' feet
	 Women disciples
	 The woman searching for her lost coin
	 The persistent widow petitioning the
	   unjust judge
	 The sorrowful women along the way
	   to the cross
		1:5-25,39-45,57-66
		 1:26-56; 2:1-20,41-52
		 2:36-38
		 7:11,12
		 7:36-50
		 8:1-3
		 15:8-10
		 18:1-8
		
		 23:27

Concern for the poor/warnings to the rich	Blessings on the poor Woes on the rich The rich fool The rich man and the beggar Lazarus	6:20-23 6:24-26 12:16-20 16:19-31
Concern for social outcasts	Shepherds Samaritans Tax agents and "sinners" Gentiles/all people	2:8-20 10:25-37; 17:11-19 15:1 2:32; 24:47

The Christian life	Gratitude and joy
	
	 Prayer
	 Proper use of material possessions
	
	 Changed social behavior in imitation
	   of God
	 Repentance/faith
		1:46-55,68-79; 2:14; 15:7,10,
		   24,32; 17:16,18; 24:53
		 3:21; 6:12; 9:18; 11:1-13; 18:1-14
		 6:32-36; 10:27-37; 12:32-
		 34;16:1-13
		 9:3-5,16; 10:2-16,38-42; 12:41-
		   48; 22:24-27
		 3:7-14; 5:32; 10:13; 11:32;
		   13:3-5; 15:7-10; 24:47

MAPS

CONTEMPORARY MAPS

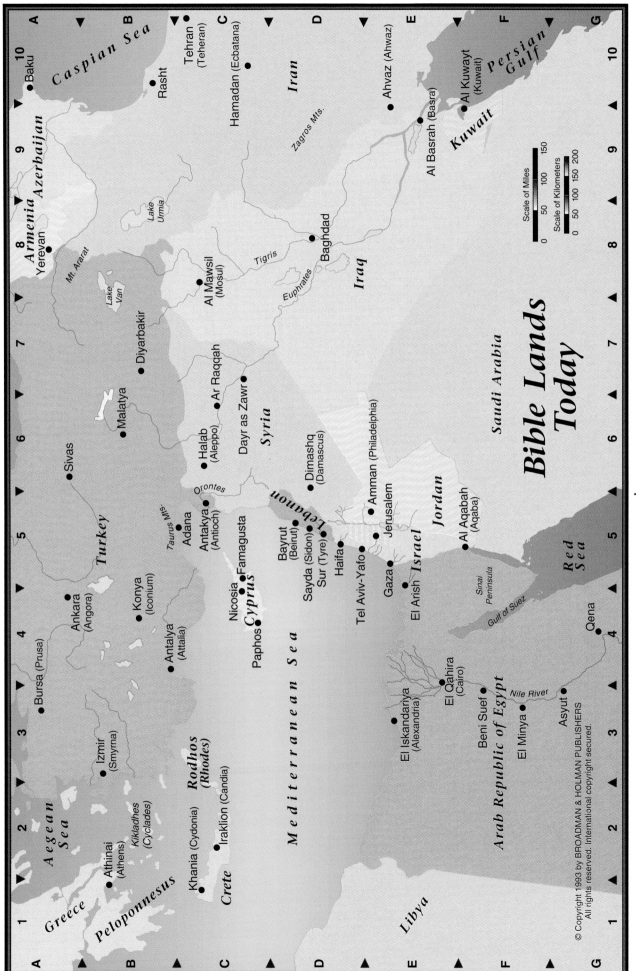

Bible Lands Today

-107-

WORLD A: THE UNREACHED WORLD

World A is made up of all people who have never heard about the saving power of Jesus Christ because they have not had access to the gospel. It is the unreached world.

Who are these unreached? Consider the following illustration. Imagine you live in a world of four people. You have plenty of food, but the other three people are starving. You see two of them going down a road and, recognizing their plight, you tell them where they can find a storehouse filled with good things to eat. The other person is on a different path. In fact, without knowing it, he is walking away from both you and the storehouse that contains the only nourishment capable of saving him.

The other person, in terms of spiritual salvation, is World A. In real life, he represents approximately 1.2 billion people—one-fourth of humanity—people groups in which one out of every two individuals has neither heard nor has had the opportunity to hear the gospel of Jesus Christ. Researchers estimate that 85 percent of these unreached individuals in our world live in the large green band shown on the map below extending through North Africa and Central Asia. He will perish, not because he has rejected Christ, but because he has no understanding of what Christ has offered. He has not been reached with any communication about the Christian hope of salvation.

The following statistics represent the urgency of the global Christian mission endeavor:

Christians spend 99.9% of Christian income on themselves, 0.09% on World B, also referred to as the evangelized non-Christian world, and 0.01% on World A, the unevangelized world.

The same percentage breakdown (99.9, 0.09, 0.01) is applicable when considering money provided specifically for "Christian" purposes.

Approximately 99% of all Christian literature is consumed by World C; approximately 0.1% is produced for World A.

Only 1% of all Scripture distribution occurs in World A; 62% of Scripture distribution occurs in World C.

Approximately 3,000 foreign missionaries target populations in World A; nearly 260,000 foreign missionaries are sent out to other countries considered to be in World C.

Comparison of resources for

World A
World B
World C

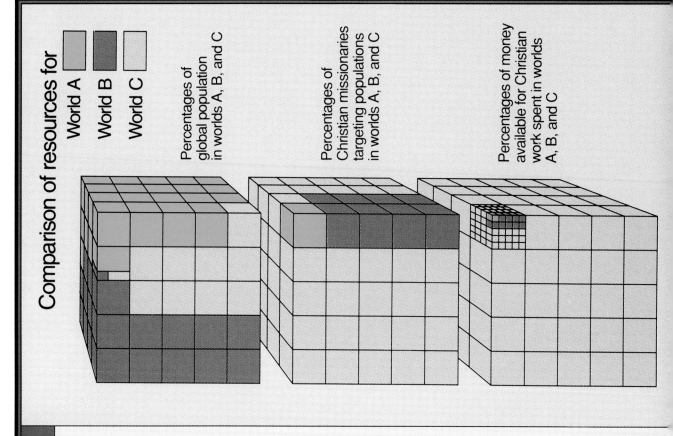

Percentages of global population in worlds A, B, and C

Percentages of Christian missionaries targeting populations in worlds A, B, and C

Percentages of money available for Christian work spent in worlds A, B, and C

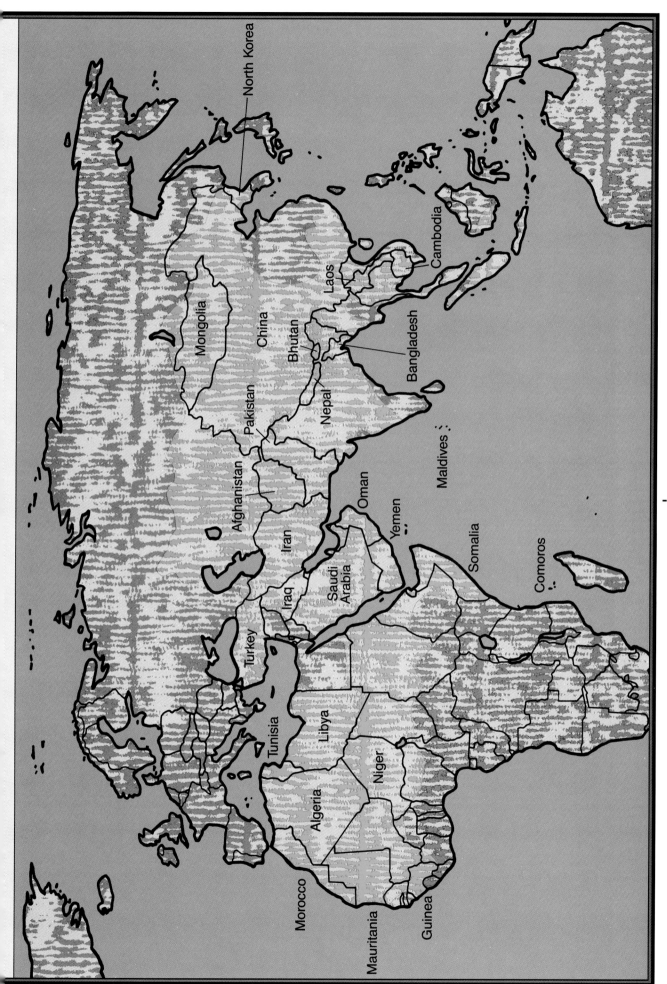

North Korea

Mongolia

China

Laos

Cambodia

Bhutan

Bangladesh

Pakistan

Nepal

Afghanistan

Oman

Maldives

Iran

Yemen

Saudi
Arabia

Somalia

Iraq

Comoros

Turkey

Tunisia

Libya

Niger

Algeria

Morocco

Mauritania

Guinea

-109-

OLD TESTAMENT MAPS

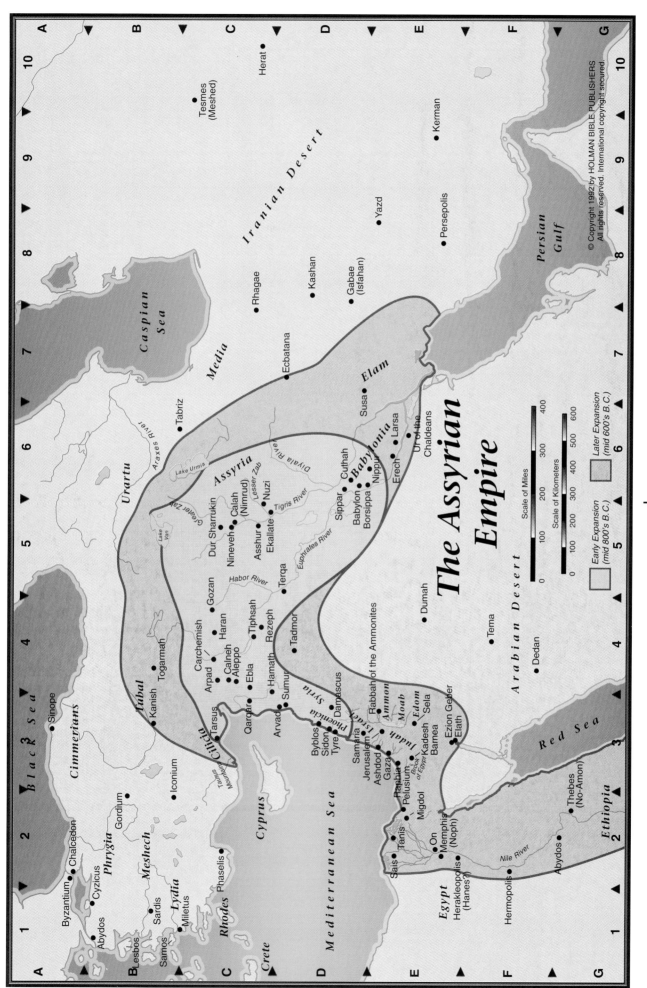

The Assyrian Empire

Scale of Miles
0   100   200   300   400

Scale of Kilometers
0   100   200   300   400   500   600

Early Expansion
(mid 800's B.C.)

Later Expansion
(mid 600's B.C.)

MAPS

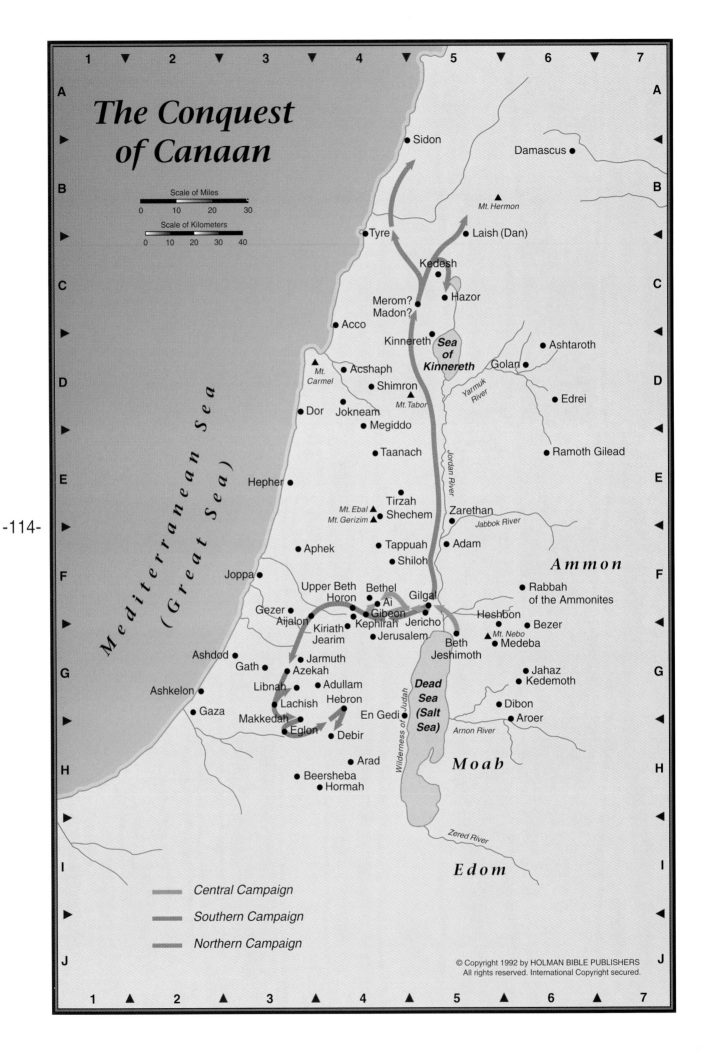

The Conquest of Canaan

Scale of Miles
0   10   20   30

Scale of Kilometers
0   10   20   30   40

M
A
P
S

Central Campaign

Southern Campaign

Northern Campaign

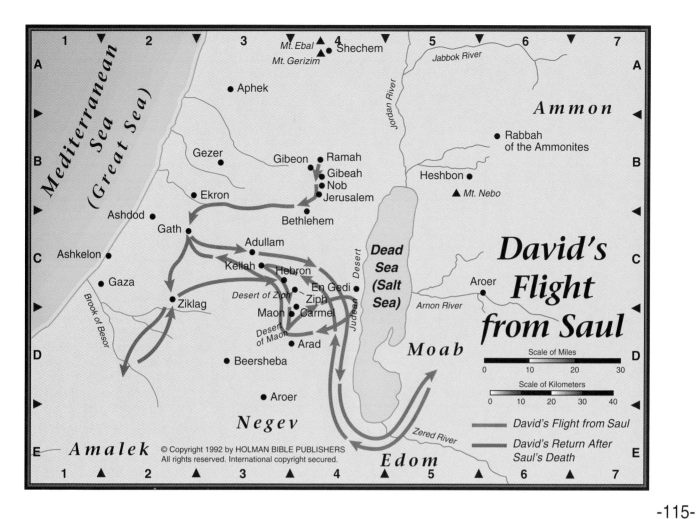

David's Flight from Saul

Mediterranean Sea (Great Sea)

Ammon

Mt. Ebal
Shechem
Mt. Gerizim
Jabbok River
Jordan River
Aphek
Rabbah of the Ammonites
Gezer
Gibeon
Ramah
Gibeah
Nob
Heshbon
Mt. Nebo
Ekron
Jerusalem
Ashdod
Bethlehem
Gath
Adullam
Dead Sea (Salt Sea)
Ashkelon
Keilah
Hebron
Gaza
Desert of Ziph
En Gedi
Judean Desert
Aroer
Ziklag
Ziph
Arnon River
Maon
Carmel
Moab
Brook of Besor
Desert of Maon
Arad
Beersheba
Aroer
Negev
Zered River
Amalek
Edom

Scale of Miles
0 10 20 30

Scale of Kilometers
0 10 20 30 40

David's Flight from Saul
David's Return After Saul's Death

-115-

MAPS

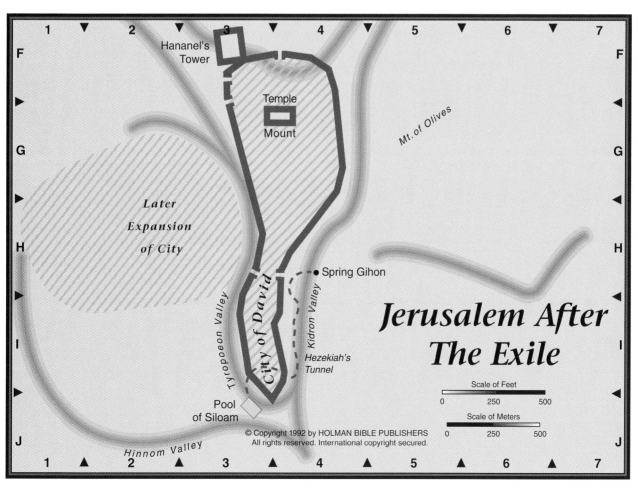

Jerusalem After The Exile

Hananel's Tower
Temple Mount
Mt. of Olives
Later Expansion of City
Spring Gihon
Tyropoeon Valley
City of David
Kidron Valley
Hezekiah's Tunnel
Pool of Siloam
Hinnom Valley

Scale of Feet
0 250 500

Scale of Meters
0 250 500

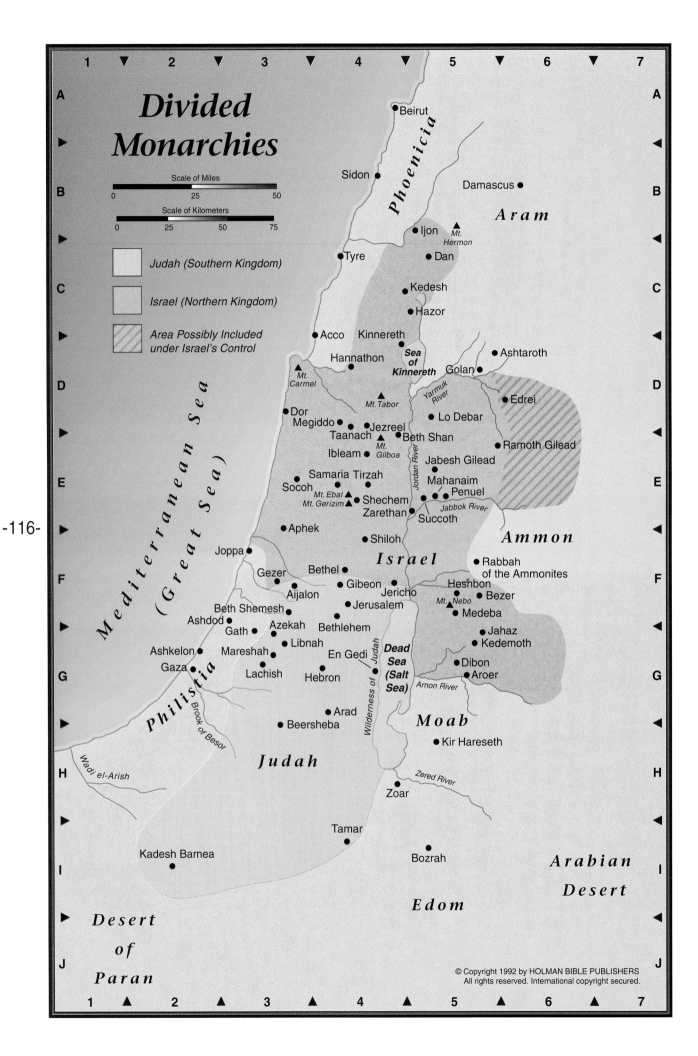

Divided Monarchies

Scale of Miles

0   25   50

Scale of Kilometers

0   25   50   75

Judah (Southern Kingdom)

Israel (Northern Kingdom)

Area Possibly Included
under Israel's Control

Phoenicia

Aram

Beirut

Sidon

Damascus •

Ijon
Mt. Hermon ▲

Tyre

Dan

Kedesh

Hazor

Acco

Kinnereth

Ashtaroth •

Hannathon

Sea of Kinnereth

Golan

Mt. Carmel ▲

Yarmuk River

Edrei

Dor

Mt. Tabor ▲

Lo Debar

Megiddo

Jezreel

Beth Shan

Ramoth Gilead

Taanach ▲
Mt. Gilboa

Jabesh Gilead

Ibleam

Samaria   Tirzah

Mahanaim

Socoh

Mt. Ebal ▲

Penuel

Jordan River

Mt. Gerizim ▲   Shechem

Zarethan

Jabbok River

Succoth

Ammon

Aphek

Shiloh

Israel

Joppa •

Rabbah
of the Ammonites

Gezer

Bethel

Gibeon

Heshbon

Aijalon

Jericho

Bezer

Beth Shemesh

Jerusalem

Mt. Nebo ▲

Medeba

Ashdod •

Gath

Azekah

Bethlehem

Jahaz

Libnah

Kedemoth

Ashkelon •

Mareshah

En Gedi

Dead Sea (Salt Sea)

Dibon

Gaza •

Lachish

Hebron

Wilderness of Judah

Aroer

Philistia

Arnon River

Moab

Brook of Besor

Arad

Beersheba

Kir Hareseth •

Judah

Wadi el-Arish

Zered River

Zoar

Tamar

Kadesh Barnea •

Bozrah •

Arabian Desert

Edom

Desert

of

Paran

Mediterranean Sea (Great Sea)

M
A
P
S

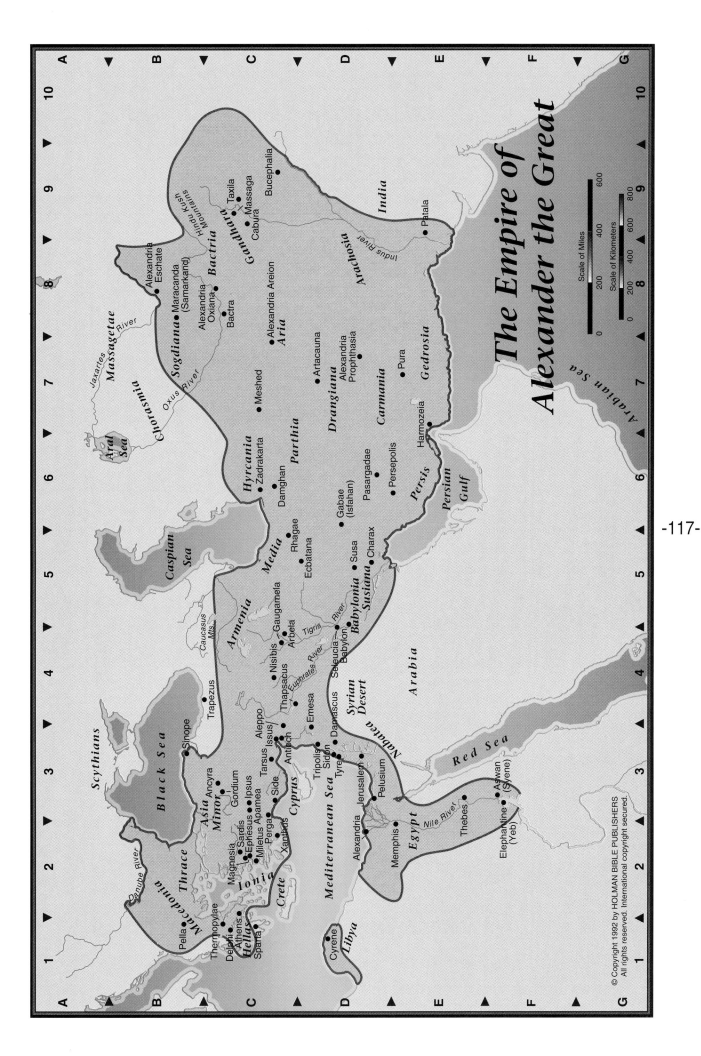

The Empire of Alexander the Great

-117-

MAPS

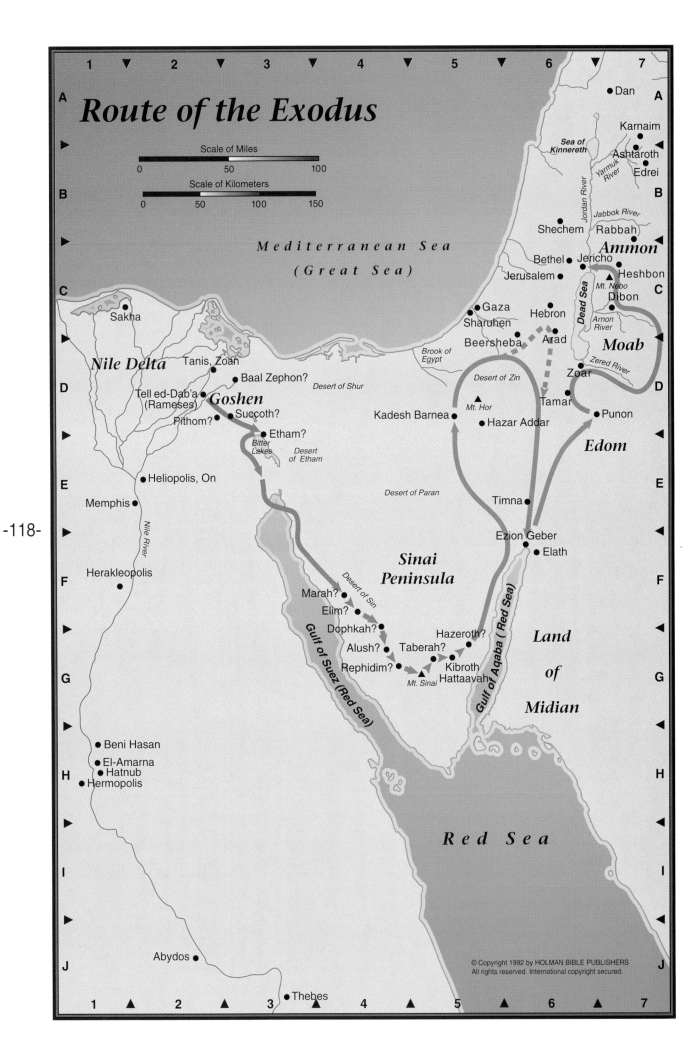

Route of the Exodus

Scale of Miles

Scale of Kilometers

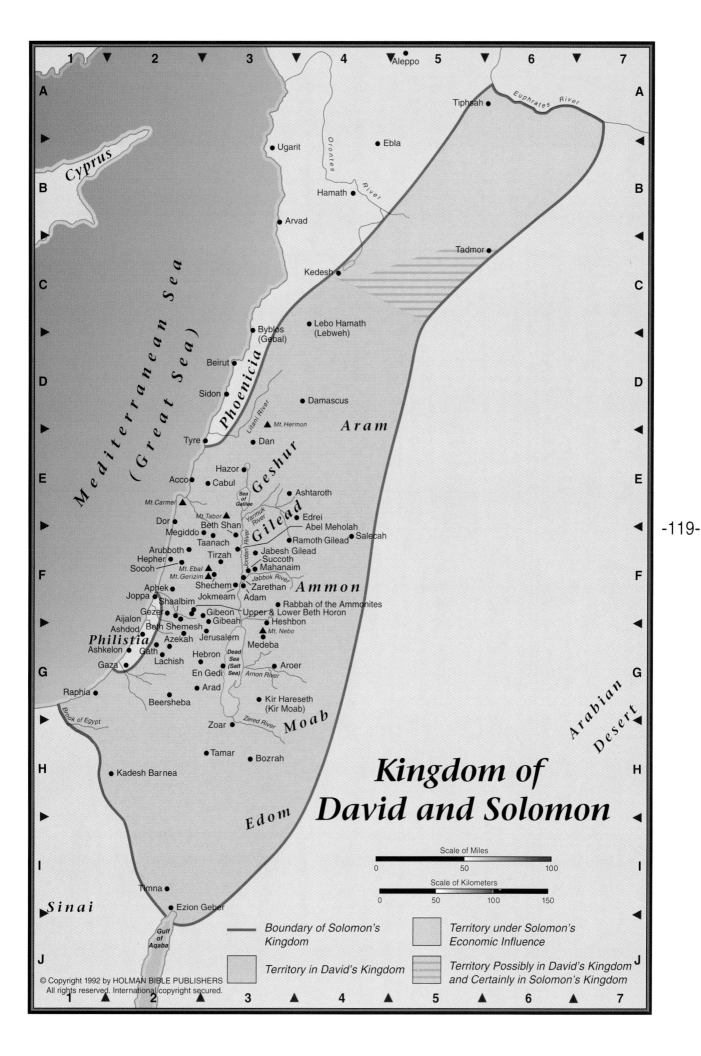

Kingdom of David and Solomon

-119-

**M
A
P
S**

Cyprus

*Mediterranean Sea
(Great Sea)*

Ugarit
Ebla
Tiphsah •
Euphrates River

Orontes River

Hamath
Arvad
Kedesh •
Tadmor •

Byblos (Gebal)
Lebo Hamath (Lebweh)

Beirut
Sidon

Damascus •
Aram

Tyre
Dan
▲ *Mt. Hermon*
Litani River

Phoenicia

Acco •
Hazor •
Cabul •
Geshur

Ashtaroth •

Mt. Carmel ▲
Sea of Galilee
Edrei •
Gilead
Abel Meholah
Salecah •

Dor •
Mt. Tabor ▲
Beth Shan
Ramoth Gilead •
Yarmuk River

Megiddo •
Taanach •
Jordan River
Jabesh Gilead •
Succoth •

Arubboth •
Tirzah •
Mahanaim •

Hepher •
Socoh •
Mt. Ebal ▲
Mt. Gerizim ▲
Jabbok River
Ammon

Aphek •
Shechem •
Zarethan •

Joppa •
Shaalbim •
Jokmeam •
Adam •

Gezer •
Gibeon •
Rabbah of the Ammonites •

Aijalon •
Upper & Lower Beth Horon
Heshbon •

Ashdod •
Beth Shemesh •
Gibeah •
▲ *Mt. Nebo*

Philistia
Azekah •
Jerusalem •
Medeba •

Ashkelon •
Gath •
Hebron •
Dead Sea (Salt Sea)

Gaza •
Lachish •
Aroer •

En Gedi •
Arnon River

Raphia •
Arad •

Brook of Egypt
Beersheba •
Kir Hareseth (Kir Moab) •

Zoar •
Zered River
Moab

Tamar •
Bozrah •

Arabian Desert

Kadesh Barnea •

Edom

Sinai

Timna •
Ezion Geber •

Gulf of Aqaba

Scale of Miles
0   50   100

Scale of Kilometers
0   50   100   150

——— Boundary of Solomon's Kingdom

▭ Territory in David's Kingdom

▭ Territory under Solomon's Economic Influence

▭ Territory Possibly in David's Kingdom and Certainly in Solomon's Kingdom

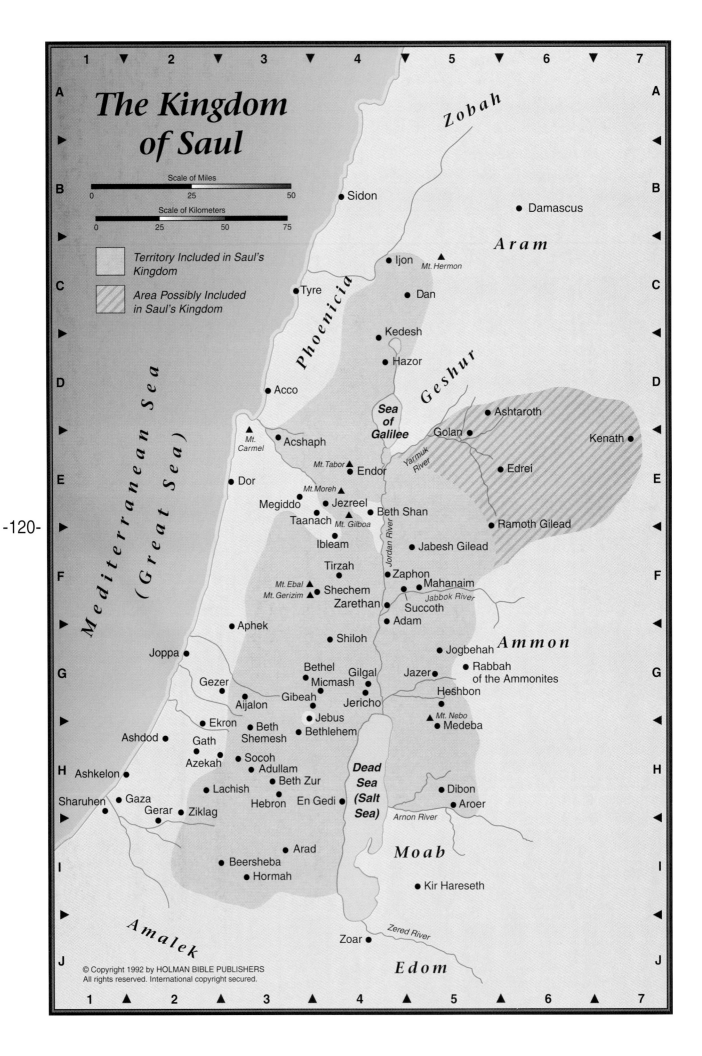

The Kingdom of Saul

Scale of Miles
0   25   50

Scale of Kilometers
0   25   50   75

Territory Included in Saul's Kingdom

Area Possibly Included in Saul's Kingdom

Zobah

Aram

Phoenicia

Geshur

Mediterranean Sea (Great Sea)

Sea of Galilee

Dead Sea (Salt Sea)

Ammon

Moab

Amalek

Edom

• Sidon
• Damascus
• Ijon   ▲ Mt. Hermon
• Tyre
• Dan
• Kedesh
• Hazor
• Acco
▲ Mt. Carmel
• Acshaph
• Ashtaroth
• Golan
• Kenath
• Dor
Mt. Tabor ▲ • Endor
• Edrei
Mt. Moreh ▲
• Megiddo   • Jezreel
• Beth Shan
• Taanach ▲ Mt. Gilboa
• Ramoth Gilead
• Ibleam
• Jabesh Gilead
• Tirzah
• Zaphon
Jordan River
Yarmuk River
Mt. Ebal ▲   • Mahanaim
Mt. Gerizim ▲ • Shechem
Jabbok River
• Zarethan
• Succoth
• Aphek
• Adam
• Shiloh
• Jogbehah
• Bethel   • Gilgal
• Jazer   • Rabbah of the Ammonites
• Micmash
• Joppa
• Gezer
• Gibeah   • Jericho
• Heshbon
• Aijalon
▲ Mt. Nebo
• Ekron   • Jebus   • Medeba
• Beth Shemesh   • Bethlehem
• Ashdod   • Gath
• Socoh
• Azekah   • Adullam
• Ashkelon   • Lachish   • Beth Zur
• Dibon
• Sharuhen   • Gaza   • Hebron   • En Gedi   • Aroer
Arnon River
• Gerar   • Ziklag
• Arad
• Beersheba
• Hormah
• Kir Hareseth
Zered River
• Zoar

-120-

M A P S

1   2   3   4   5   6   7
A   B   C   D   E   F   G   H   I   J

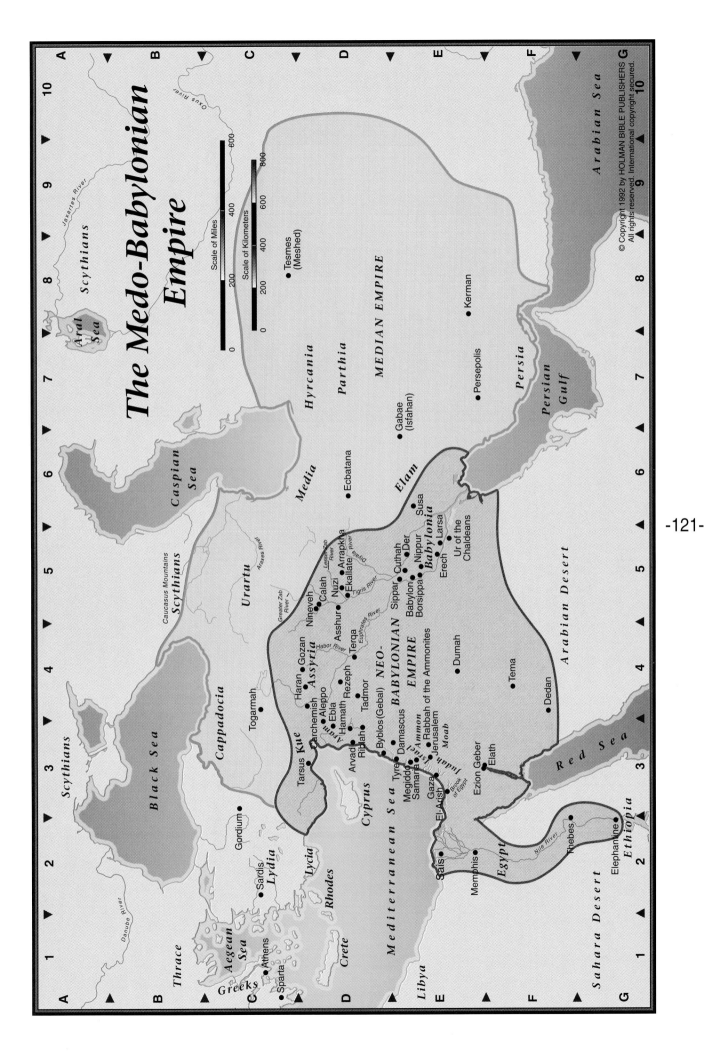

The Medo-Babylonian Empire

Scale of Miles
0   200   400   600

Scale of Kilometers
0   200   400   600   800

Scythians

Oxus River

Jaxartes River

Aral Sea

Scythians

Caspian Sea

MEDIAN EMPIRE

Tesmes (Meshed)

Hyrcania

Parthia

Media

• Ecbatana

Elam

Gabae (Isfahan)

Persia

Kerman •

Persepolis •

Persian Gulf

Arabian Sea

Caucasus Mountains

Scythians

Urartu

Araxes River

Black Sea

Greater Zab River

Lesser Zab River

Nineveh

Calah

Arrapkha

Nuzi

Ekallate

Diyala River

Der

Cuthah

Sippar

Susa

Babylon

Nippur

Larsa

Borsippa

Babylonia

Erech

Ur of the Chaldeans

Cappadocia

Togarmah •

Asshur

Terqa

Habor River

Tigris River

Euphrates River

Haran

Gozan

Assyria

Aleppo

Ebla

Rezeph

Carchemish

Hamath

Tadmor

NEO-
BABYLONIAN
EMPIRE

Rabbah of the Ammonites

Dumah •

Arabian Desert

Kue

Tarsus

Arpad

Arvad

Riblah

Byblos (Gebal)

Damascus

Ammon

Tyre

Israel

Jerusalem

Judah

Moab

Tema •

Dedan •

Gordium •

Lydia

Sardis •

Sparta •

Lycia

Rhodes

Cyprus

Mediterranean Sea

Megiddo

Samaria

Gaza

El Arish

Brook of Egypt

Ezion Geber

Elath

Red Sea

Aegean Sea

Athens •

Thrace

Greeks

Crete

Libya

Egypt

Sais •

Memphis •

Nile River

Thebes •

Elephantine •

Ethiopia

Sahara Desert

A B C D E F G

1 2 3 4 5 6 7 8 9 10

-121-

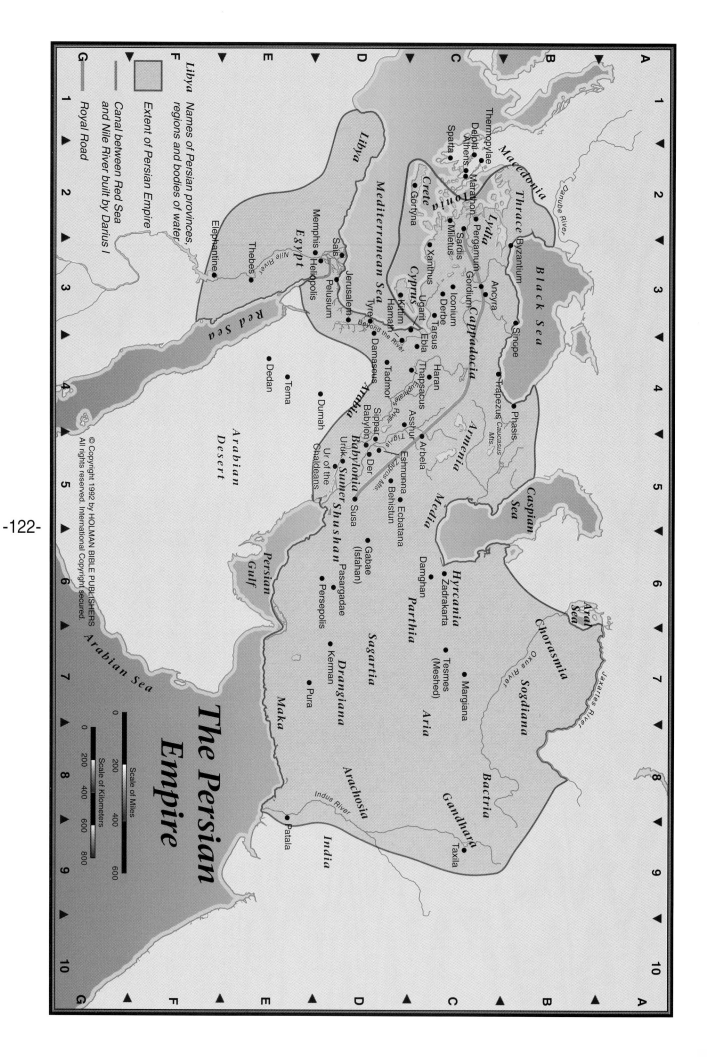

The Persian Empire

Libya Names of Persian provinces, regions and bodies of water.

Extent of Persian Empire

Canal between Red Sea and Nile River built by Darius I

Royal Road

Scale of Miles
0   200   400   600

Scale of Kilometers
0   200   400   600   800

Mediterranean Sea
Black Sea
Caspian Sea
Aral Sea
Red Sea
Persian Gulf
Arabian Sea
Arabian Desert

Macedonia
Thrace
Ionia
Lydia
Crete
Cyprus
Cappadocia
Armenia
Media
Parthia
Hyrcania
Chorasmia
Sogdiana
Bactria
Gandhara
Aria
Arachosia
Drangiana
Sagartia
India
Maka
Shushan
Sumer
Babylonia
Arabia
Egypt
Libya

Danube River
Oxus River
Jaxartes River
Indus River
Nile River
Euphrates River
Tigris R.
Zagros Mts.
Caucasus Mts.

Thermopylae
Delphi
Athens
Sparta
Marathon
Pergamum
Sardis
Miletus
Gortyna
Xanthus
Byzantium
Ancyra
Gordium
Iconium
Derbe
Tarsus
Ugarit
Kittim
Ebla
Haran
Thapsacus
Sinope
Trapezus
Phasis
Asshur
Arbela
Eshnunna
Ecbatana
Behistun
Damghan
Zadrakarta
Margiana
Tesmes (Meshed)
Memphis
Sais
Heliopolis
Pelusium
Jerusalem
Tyre
Damascus
Hamath
Tadmor
Beyond the River
Sippar
Babylon
Der
Uruk
Ur of the Chaldeans
Susa
Gabae (Isfahan)
Pasargadae
Persepolis
Kerman
Pura
Patala
Taxila
Elephantine
Thebes
Dedan
Tema
Dumah

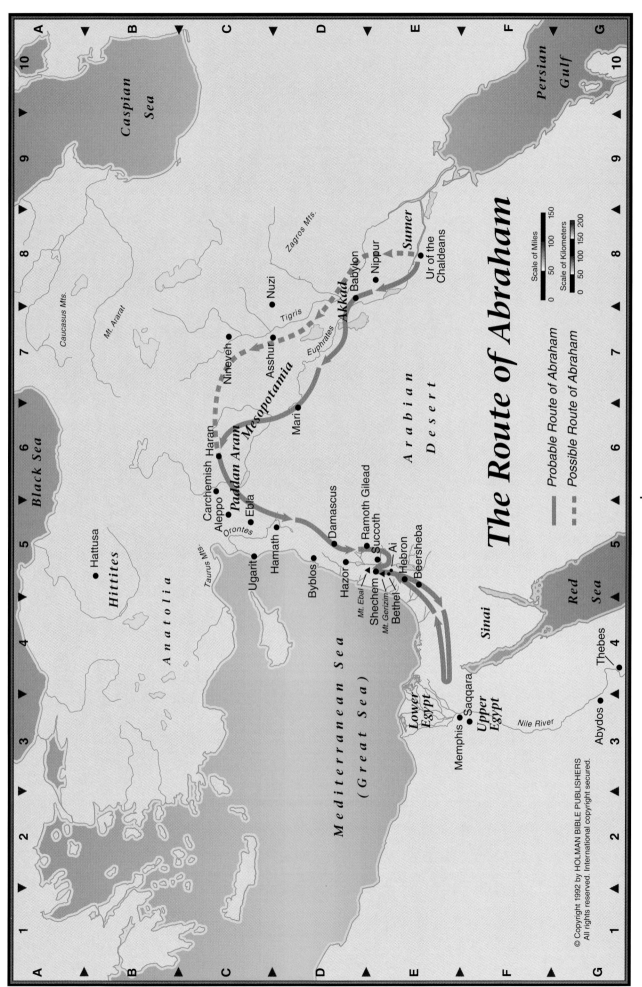

The Route of Abraham

Scale of Miles
0   50   100   150

Scale of Kilometers
0   50   100   150   200

—— Probable Route of Abraham
- - - Possible Route of Abraham

MAPS

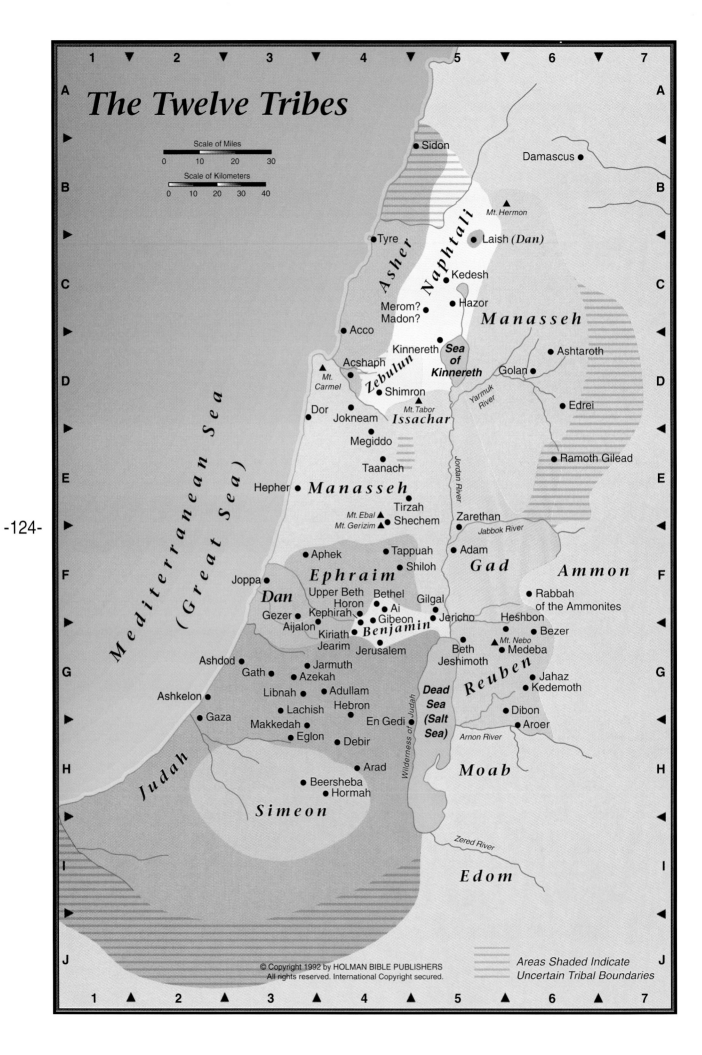

The Twelve Tribes

Scale of Miles
0 10 20 30

Scale of Kilometers
0 10 20 30 40

Sidon

Damascus

Mt. Hermon

Tyre

Laish (Dan)

Asher

Naphtali

Kedesh

Merom?
Madon?

Hazor

Manasseh

Acco

Ashtaroth

Kinnereth

Sea of Kinnereth

Golan

Acshaph

Zebulun

Mt. Carmel

Shimron

Yarmuk River

Edrei

Dor

Jo_kneam

Mt. Tabor

Issachar

Jordan River

Megiddo

Taanach

Ramoth Gilead

Hepher

Manasseh

Mediterranean Sea (Great Sea)

Tirzah

Mt. Ebal

Shechem

Zarethan

Mt. Gerizim

Jabbok River

Aphek

Tappuah

Adam

Shiloh

Gad

Ammon

Ephraim

Joppa

Dan

Upper Beth Horon

Bethel

Ai

Gilgal

Rabbah of the Ammonites

Gezer

Kephirah

Gibeon

Jericho

Heshbon

Aijalon

Benjamin

Bezer

Kiriath Jearim

Jerusalem

Beth Jeshimoth

Mt. Nebo

Medeba

Ashdod

Jarmuth

Reuben

Jahaz

Gath

Azekah

Dead Sea (Salt Sea)

Kedemoth

Ashkelon

Libnah

Adullam

Hebron

Dibon

Gaza

Lachish

En Gedi

Wilderness of Judah

Aroer

Makkedah

Eglon

Debir

Arnon River

Arad

Judah

Moab

Beersheba

Hormah

Simeon

Zered River

Edom

Areas Shaded Indicate
Uncertain Tribal Boundaries

MAPS

NEW TESTAMENT
MAPS

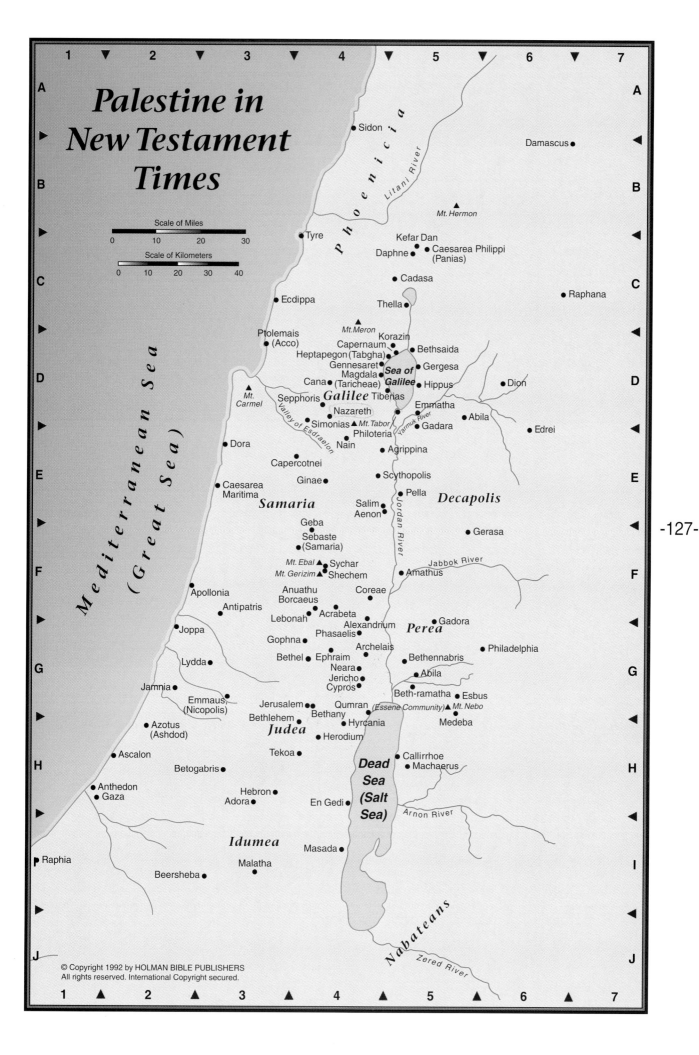

Palestine in New Testament Times

Mediterranean Sea (Great Sea)

Phoenicia

Sidon

Damascus

Mt. Hermon

Tyre

Kefar Dan

Daphne • Caesarea Philippi (Panias)

Cadasa

Raphana

Ecdippa

Thella

Ptolemais (Acco)

Mt. Meron

Korazin

Capernaum

Bethsaida

Heptapegon (Tabgha)

Gennesaret

Gergesa

Magdala (Taricheae)

Sea of Galilee

Cana

Hippus

Dion

Mt. Carmel

Sepphoris

Galilee

Tiberias

Emmatha

Nazareth

Abila

Simonias

Mt. Tabor

Gadara

Edrei

Philoteria

Nain

Agrippina

Valley of Esdraelon

Dora

Yarmuk River

Capercotnei

Ginae

Scythopolis

Jordan River

Caesarea Maritima

Pella

Decapolis

Samaria

Salim

Geba

Aenon

Sebaste (Samaria)

Gerasa

Mt. Ebal

Sychar

Jabbok River

Mt. Gerizim

Shechem

Amathus

Apollonia

Anuathu Borcaeus

Coreae

Antipatris

Acrabeta

Gadora

Lebonah

Alexandrium

Perea

Joppa

Gophna

Phasaelis

Archelais

Philadelphia

Bethel

Ephraim

Bethennabris

Lydda

Neara

Abila

Jamnia

Jericho

Cypros

Beth-ramatha

Esbus

Emmaus (Nicopolis)

Jerusalem

Qumran (Essene Community)

Mt. Nebo

Bethlehem

Bethany

Medeba

Azotus (Ashdod)

Hyrcania

Judea

Herodium

Ascalon

Tekoa

Callirrhoe

Betogabris

Machaerus

Dead Sea (Salt Sea)

Anthedon

Hebron

Gaza

Adora

En Gedi

Arnon River

Idumea

Masada

Raphia

Malatha

Beersheba

Nabateans

Zered River

Scale of Miles
0 10 20 30

Scale of Kilometers
0 10 20 30 40

M A P S

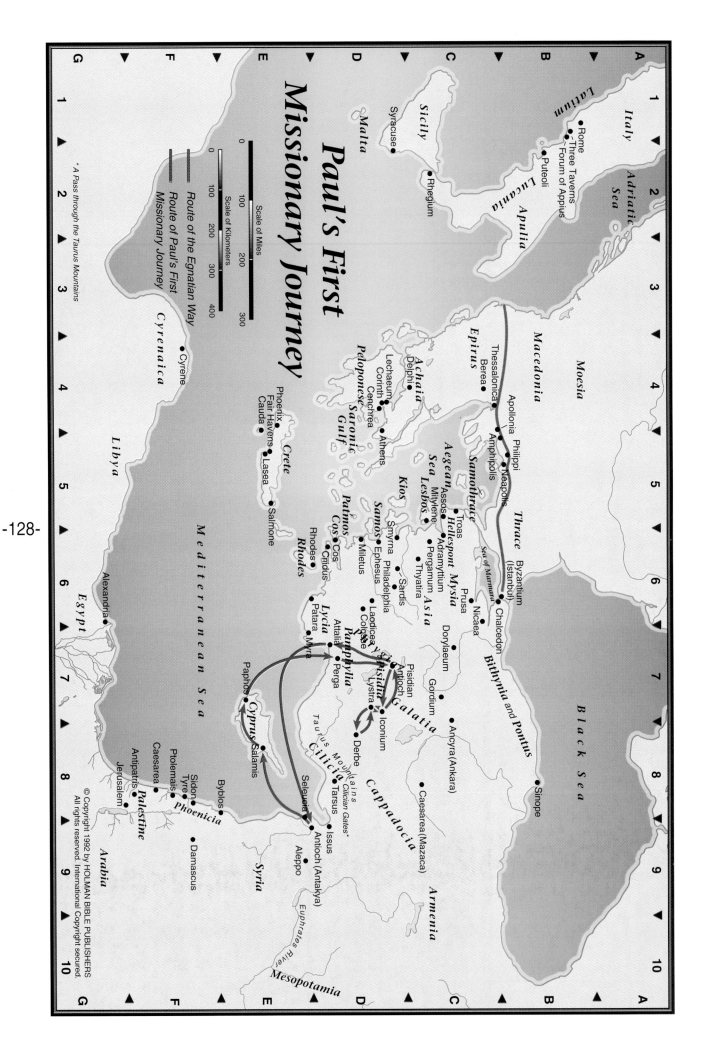

Paul's First Missionary Journey

Scale of Miles

0   100   200   300

Scale of Kilometers

0   100   200   300   400

Route of the Egnatian Way

Route of Paul's First
Missionary Journey

* A Pass through the Taurus Mountains

© Copyright 1992 by HOLMAN BIBLE PUBLISHERS
All rights reserved. International Copyright secured.

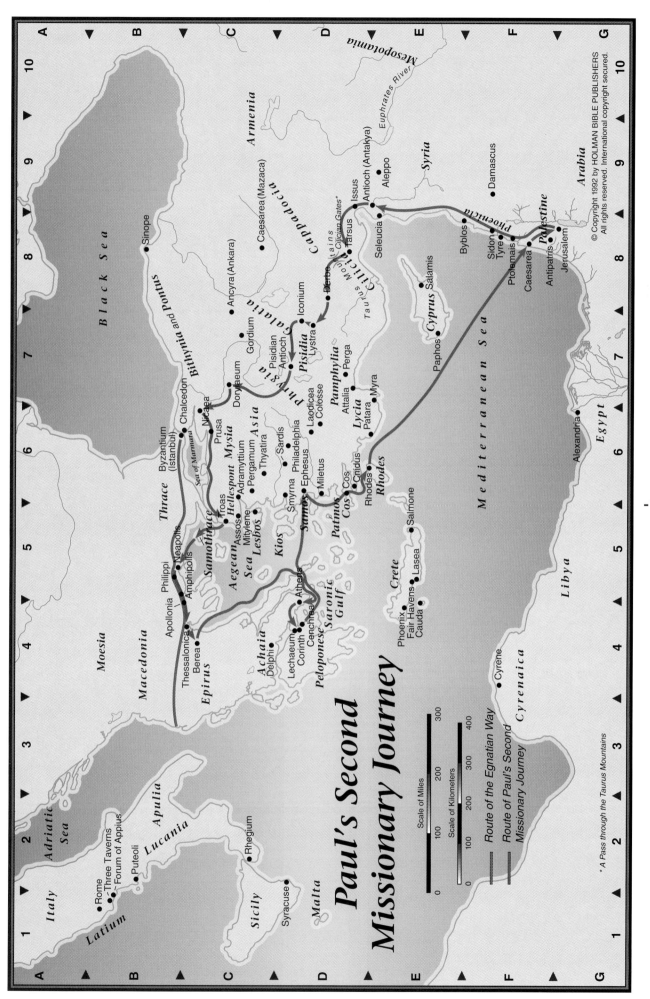

Paul's Second Missionary Journey

Scale of Miles

Scale of Kilometers

Route of the Egnatian Way

Route of Paul's Second
Missionary Journey

* A Pass through the Taurus Mountains

© Copyright 1992 by HOLMAN BIBLE PUBLISHERS
All rights reserved. International copyright secured.

-129-

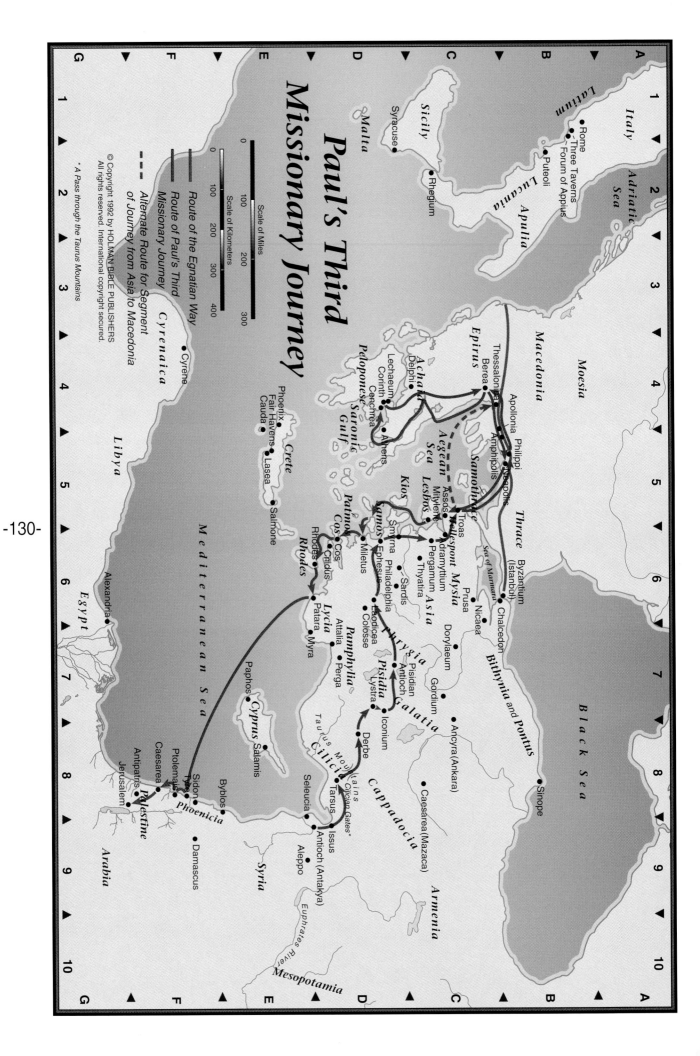

Paul's Third Missionary Journey

Scale of Miles

0   100   200   300

Scale of Kilometers

0   100   200   300   400

—— Route of the Egnatian Way

—— Route of Paul's Third Missionary Journey

- - - Alternate Route for Segment of Journey from Asia to Macedonia

* A Pass through the Taurus Mountains

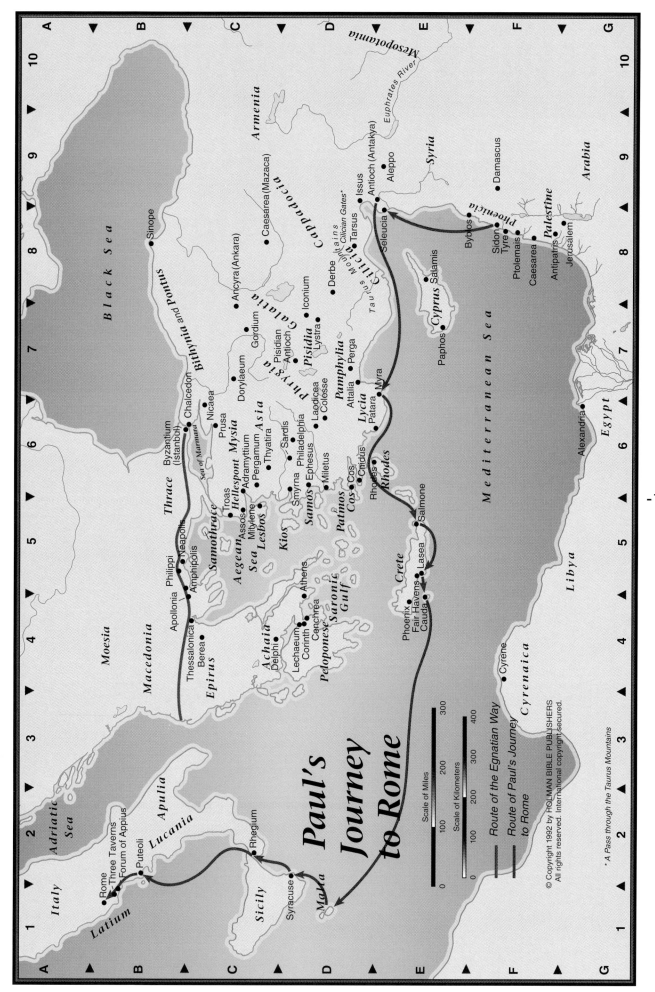

Paul's Journey to Rome

MAPS

© Copyright 1992 by HOLMAN BIBLE PUBLISHERS
All rights reserved. International copyright secured.

Scale of Miles

Scale of Kilometers

Route of the Egnatian Way

Route of Paul's Journey to Rome

* A Pass through the Taurus Mountains

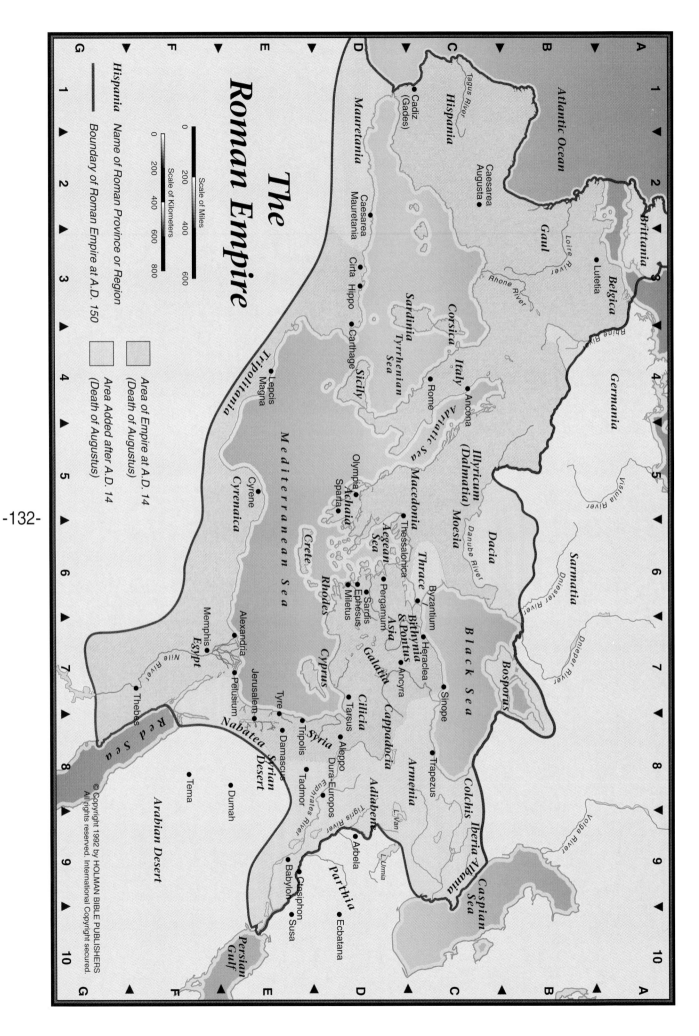

The Roman Empire

Scale of Miles
0 200 400 600

Scale of Kilometers
0 200 400 600 800

Hispania — Name of Roman Province or Region

——— Boundary of Roman Empire at A.D. 150

Area of Empire at A.D. 14
(Death of Augustus)

Area Added after A. D. 14
(Death of Augustus)

Atlantic Ocean

Brittania

Hispania

Cadiz
(Gades)

Caesarea
Augusta

Tagus River

Gaul

Belgica

Lutetia

Loire River

Rhone River

Rhine River

Germania

Visula River

Dniester River

Dnieper River

Sarmatia

Mauretania

Caesarea
Mauretania

Cirta
Hippo

Carthage

Sardinia

Corsica

Tyrrhenian
Sea

Sicily

Italy

Rome

Ancona

Adriatic Sea

Illyricum
(Dalmatia)

Moesia

Dacia

Danube River

Macedonia

Thessalonica

Thrace

Byzantium

Bithynia
& Pontus

Heraclea

Ancyra

Black Sea

Bosporus

Colchis

Iberia

Albania

Caspian Sea

Volga River

Tripolitania

Lepcis
Magna

Cyrene

Cyrenaica

Mediterranean Sea

Crete

Olympia

Sparta

Achaia

Aegean
Sea

Pergamum

Sardis

Ephesus

Miletus

Asia

Galatia

Cappadocia

Sinope

Trapezus

Armenia

Adiabene

L. Van

L. Urmia

Rhodes

Cyprus

Cilicia

Tarsus

Syria

Aleppo

Dura-Europos

Euphrates River

Tigris River

Arbela

Parthia

Ecbatana

Susa

Babylon

Ctesiphon

Persian
Gulf

Memphis

Alexandria

Pelusium

Egypt

Nile River

Thebes

Jerusalem

Tyre

Tripolis

Damascus

Tadmor

Nabatea

Syrian
Desert

Dumah

Tema

Red Sea

Arabian Desert

© Copyright 1992 by HOLMAN BIBLE PUBLISHERS
All rights reserved. International Copyright secured.

A B C D E F G

1 2 3 4 5 6 7 8 9 10

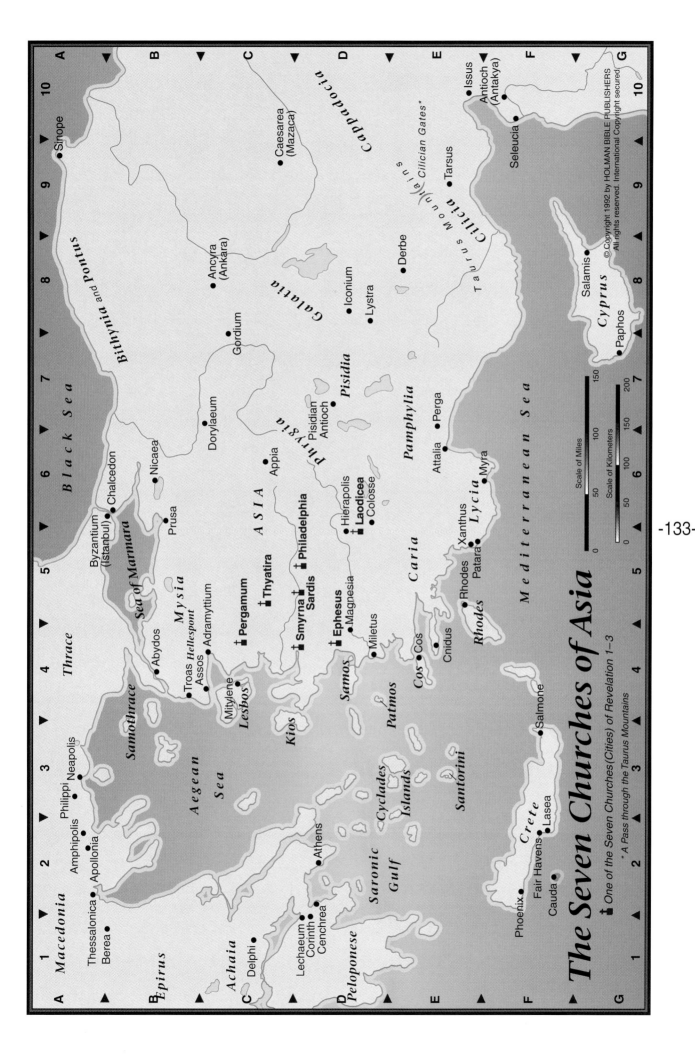

The Seven Churches of Asia

☩ One of the Seven Churches (Cities) of Revelation 1–3

*A Pass through the Taurus Mountains

Scale of Miles

Scale of Kilometers

-133-

MAPS

RECONSTRUCTIONS

OLD TESTAMENT RECONSTRUCTIONS

Reconstruction of the Ark of the Covenant drawn in the Egyptian style, reflecting 400 years of captive influence in Egyptian bondage.

-139-

Reconstruction of an eighth-century B.C. Israelite house, showing rooms for sleeping on straw mats and for storage. The outer courtyard was used for food preparation, cooking, and to house small animals. Construction of houses did not change much over the centuries until the New Testament period. So, this was a typical pattern for the average home of the Old Testament period.

RECONSTRUCTIONS

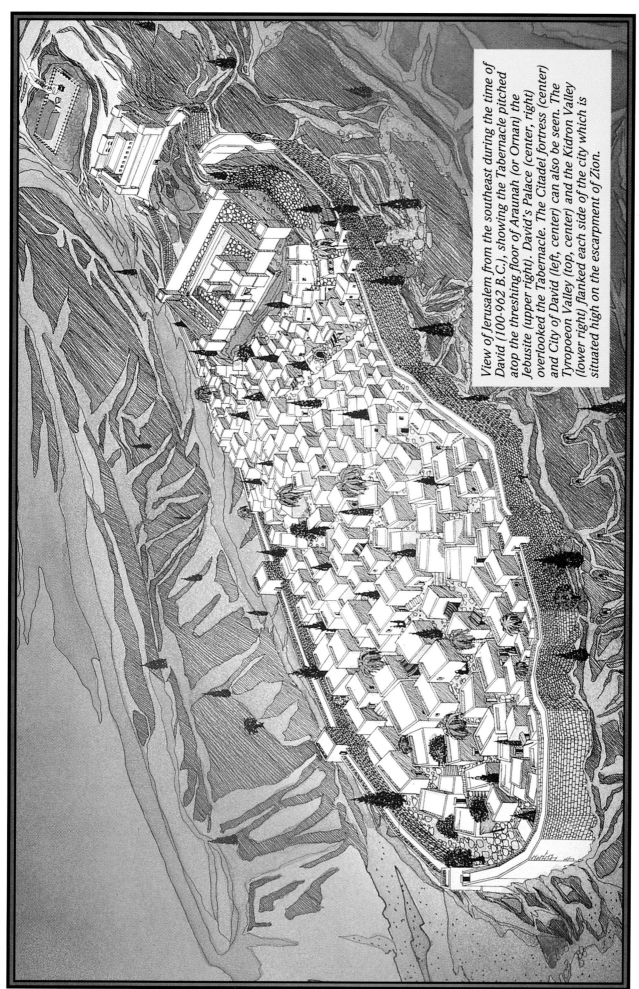

View of Jerusalem from the southeast during the time of David (100-962 B.C.), showing the Tabernacle pitched atop the threshing floor of Araunah (or Ornan) the Jebusite (upper right). David's Palace (center, right) overlooked the Tabernacle. The Citadel fortress (center) and City of David (left, center) can also be seen. The Tyropoeon Valley (top, center) and the Kidron Valley (lower right) flanked each side of the city which is situated high on the escarpment of Zion.

-141-

Reconstruction of Solomon's Temple (957-587 B.C.) at Jerusalem and its courts. Shown are the ten lavers (five on each side of the Temple), the Molten Sea (lower, center), and the Altar of Burnt Offerings (center). Solomon's palace (left) stood immediately west of the Temple court, overlooking the Temple.

Cut-away view of Solomon's Temple at Jerusalem, showing the porch, the holy place, and the holy of holies—where giant protecting cherubim and the sacred ark of the covenant were placed.

-143-

Reconstruction of the Israelite Tabernacle and its court. The court was formed by curtains attached to erect poles. Before the tent was placed the Altar of Burnt Offerings and the Laver. The Tabernacle was always erected to face the east, so this view is from the northeast.

-144-

A ziggurat dating to the Babylonian period (605-550 B.C.).

-145-

NEW TESTAMENT RECONSTRUCTIONS

First-century Athens, Greece, as it appeared during the time of Paul. The view is from the northwest of the Agora (market, business, and civic center) of the lower city, which is in the foreground. The Acropolis (upper city) with the famous Parthenon, dedicated to the goddess Athena, is in the background. The Aeropagus (Mars Hill) where Paul addressed the citizens of Athens is at right.

Reconstruction of Caesarea Maritima where Paul was imprisoned for two years (Acts 23:31–26:32).

-149-

Cut-away reconstruction of a first-century A.D. Israelite house.

A typical synagogue of the first century A.D. showing the large inner room where the men gathered and its loft above where the women gathered. This particular drawing is patterned after the synagogue at Capernaum.

-151-

Reconstruction of a first-century wine press, showing the pressing basin with drain leading to the lower collecting basin.

Reconstruction of Herod's Temple (20 B.C.–A.D. 70) at Jerusalem as viewed from the southeast. The drawing reflects archaeological discoveries made since excavations began in 1967 along the south end of the Temple Mount platform. The staircase (left) leads up from the lower city to a gateway (not shown) at Robinson's Arch. The monumental Herodian staircase also leads up from the lower city to the Double and Triple (Huldah) Gates. View provides an overview of the outer and inner courts of the Temple precinct atop the Temple Mount.

-153-

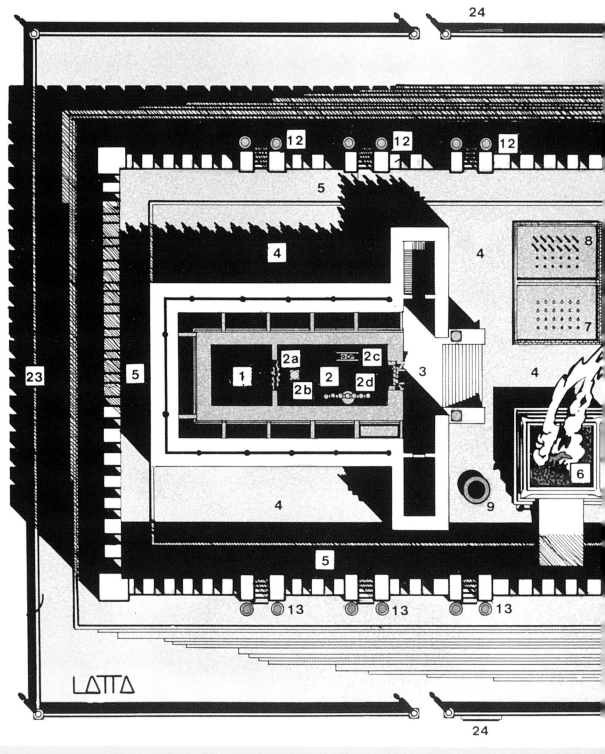

LATTA

Herod's Temple (20 B.C.–A.D. 70) was begun in the eighteenth year of King Herod the Great's reign (37–4 B.C.). According to Josephus, first-century Jewish historian, Herod's Temple was constructed after the old foundations were removed. The old edifice, Zerubbabel's Temple, was a modest restoration of the Temple of Solomon destroyed by the Babylonian conquest. The central building was completed in just two years—without any interruption of the Temple services. The surrounding buildings and spacious courts, considerably enlarged, were not completed until A.D. 64. The Temple was destroyed by the Romans under the command of Titus during the second Jewish revolt in A.D. 70.

1. Holy of Holies (where the ark of the covenant and the giant cherubim were once enshrined)
2. Holy Place
2a. Veil (actually two giant tapestries hung before the entrance of the holy of holies to allow the high priest entry between them without exposing the sacred shrine. It was this veil that was "rent" upon the death of Jesus).
2b. Altar of Incense
2c. Table of Shew Bread
2d. Seven-branched Lampstand (Great Menorah)
 3. Temple Porch

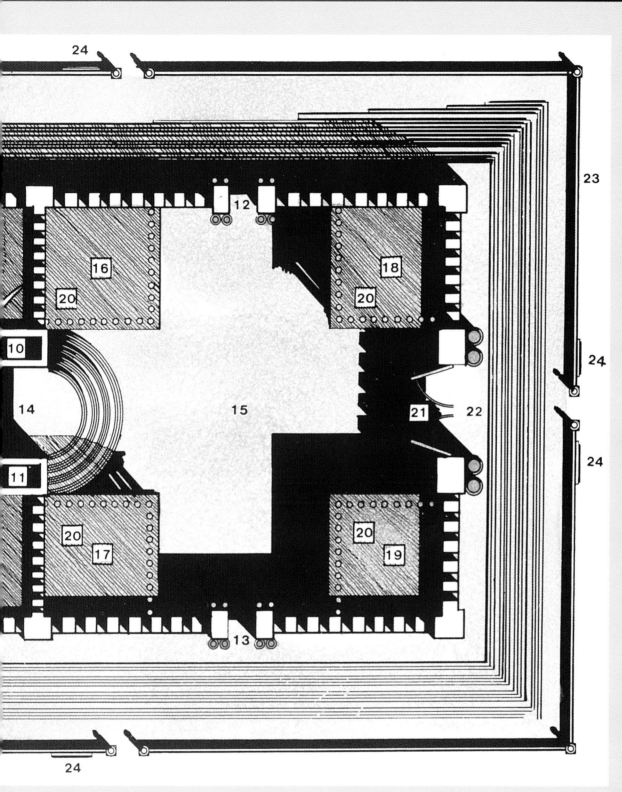

4. Court of Priests
5. Court of Israel (Men)
6. Altar of Burnt Offerings
7. Animal Tethering Area
8. Slaughtering and Skinning Area
9. Laver
10. Chamber of Phineas (storage of vestments)
11. Chamber of the Bread Maker
12. North Gates of the Inner Courts
13. South Gates of the Inner Courts
14. East (Nicanor) Gate
15. Court of Women

16. Court of Nazirites
17. Court of Woodshed
18. Lepers' Chamber
19. Shemanyah (possibly meaning "oil of Yah")
20. Women's Balconies (for viewing Temple activities)
21. Gate Beautiful (?)
22. Terrace
23. Soreg (three-cubit-high partition)
24. Warning Inscriptions to Gentiles

RECONSTRUCTIONS

Reconstruction of Herod the Great's Winter Palace at Jericho. Situated at the mouth of the Wadi (dry creek) Kelt along the lower slope of the western ridge of the Jordan valley, the palace had a commanding view of New Testament Jericho and the arid, fertile Jordan river valley.

-156-

Reconstruction of New Testament Jericho based on home, shop, and building architecture of the period.

-157-

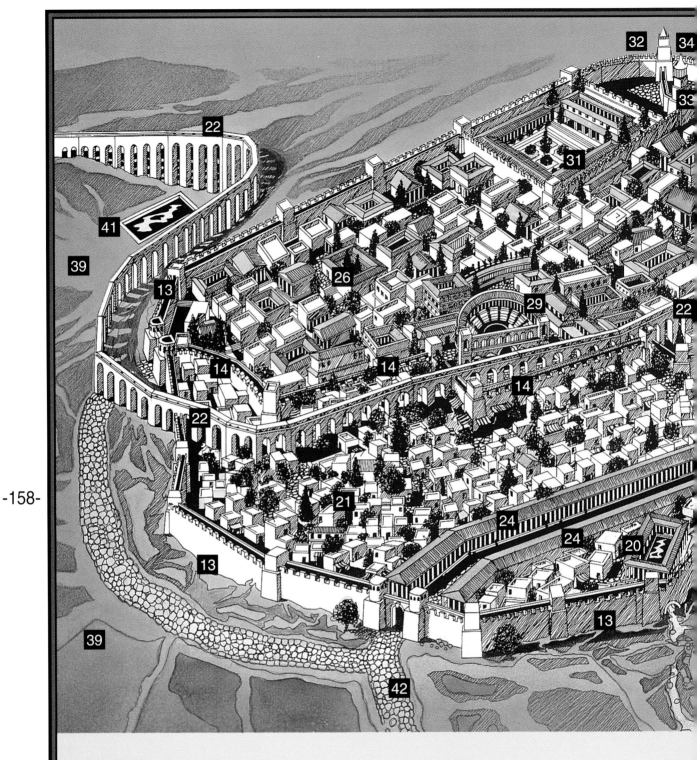

-158-

Jerusalem in the Time of Jesus
 1. The Temple (Herod's Temple)
 2. Women's Court
 3. The Soreg
 4. The Court of the Gentiles
 5. Royal Porch
 6. Eastern Gate (the present-day Golden Gate)
 7. Antonia Fortress
 8. The Double Gate (the Western Huldah Gate)
 9. The Triple Gate (the Eastern Huldah Gate)
 10. Monumental Herodian Staircase (sections still
     remain today)
 11. The City of David (established by David, the
     oldest part of the city)
 12. Earliest defense wall (destroyed and

constructed many times)
 13. Herodian outer defense wall around the
     expanded city
 14. Herodian wall separating the Upper City (or
     affluent district) from the Lower City (or lower
     economic district)
 15. The Second North Wall (possible location)
 16. Garden of Gethsemane (the west side of the
     Mount of Olives)
 17. Mount of Olives
 18. Kidron Valley
 19. Gihon Spring
 20. Pool of Siloam
 21. Tyropoeon Valley (Lower City)
 22. Herodian aqueduct (possible location)

23. Shops and marketplace of Jesus' day
24. Additional shops and marketplace (probably added at a later time)
25. Staircase (Robinson's Arch) leading up from the Lower City
26. Upper City
27. Causeway (Wilson's Arch) leading from the Upper City to the Temple
28. Residential houses
29. Roman Theater (structure mentioned by Josephus but whose location remains unverified)
30. Hippodrome (structure mentioned by Josephus but whose location remains unverified)

31. Herod's Palace
32. Phasael Tower
33. Mariamne Tower
34. Hippicus Tower
35. Sheep Pool
36. Traditional Golgotha (Calvary)
37. Traditional tomb of Jesus
38. Pool of Bethesda
39. Hinnom Valley
40. Gennath Gate
41. Serpent's Pool
42. Road to the Dead Sea
43. Road to Sebaste (Samaria)

RECONSTRUCTIONS

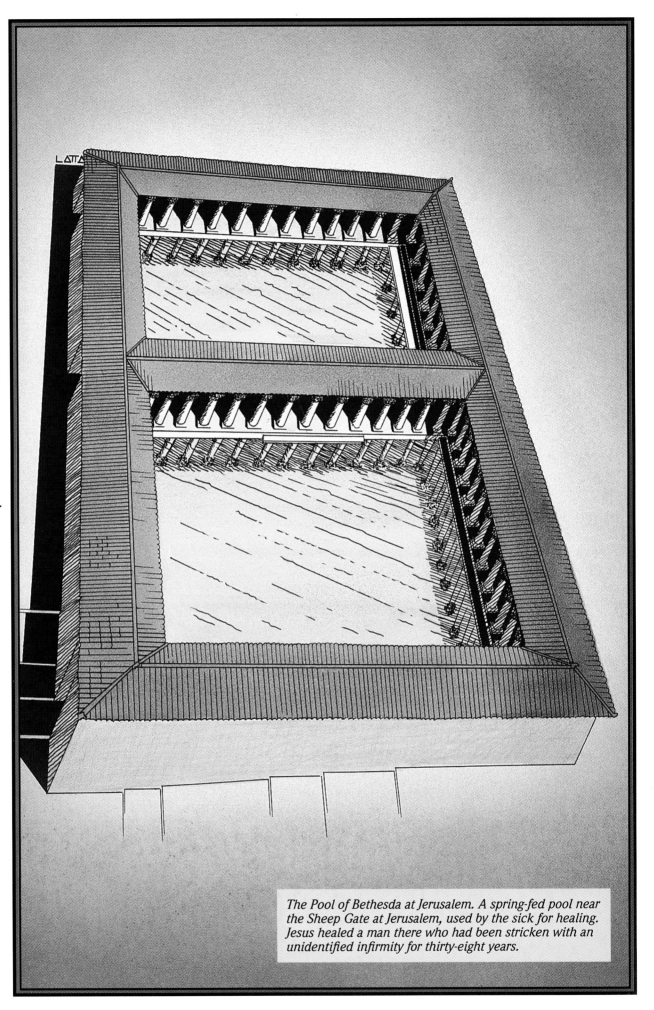

The Pool of Bethesda at Jerusalem. A spring-fed pool near the Sheep Gate at Jerusalem, used by the sick for healing. Jesus healed a man there who had been stricken with an unidentified infirmity for thirty-eight years.

RECONSTRUCTIONS

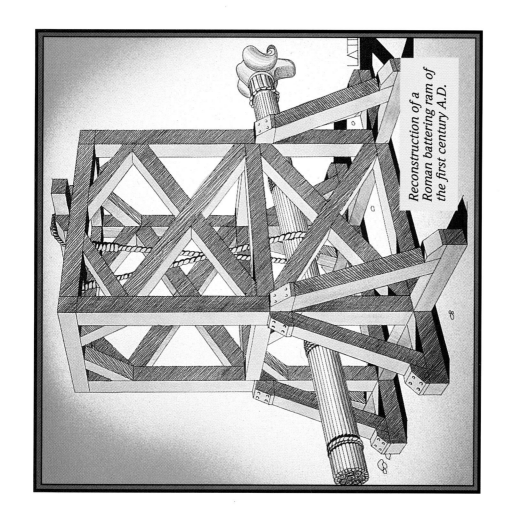

Reconstruction of a Roman battering ram of the first century A.D.

Reconstruction of an ingenious Roman archer's machine of the first century A.D.

RECONSTRUCTIONS

Reconstruction of a Roman siege tower with battering ram of the first century A.D.